MRS CAMERON'S DIARY

MRS CAMERON'S DIARY

As seen by
Catherine Bennett

virago

VIRAGO

First published in Great Britain in 2011 by Virago Press

A CIP catalogue record for this book
is available from the British Library.

ISBN 978-1-84408-776-1

Typeset by M Rules
Printed and bound in Great Britain by
Clays Ltd, St Ives plc

Papers used by Virago are from well-managed forests
and other responsible sources.

MIX
Paper from
responsible sources
FSC® C104740

Virago Press
An imprint of
Little, Brown Book Group
100 Victoria Embankment
London EC4Y 0DY

An Hachette UK Company
www.hachette.co.uk

www.virago.co.uk

This book is based on Catherine Bennett's
Guardian column in *G2*, 'Mrs Cameron's Diary'

For Rebekah

An Introduction by the Right Honourable David Cameron MP

It's an indescribable honour to introduce Sam's first-ever book – though I'm more than a little miffed that she has beaten me to it! I'll fess up: it was indeed her husband who suggested that Samantha might want to keep a diary, for her sins. And let's be honest, how big a mistake was that? I think most people know Sam as a brilliant mother and homemaker, a gifted and highly professional entrepreneur, a fantastic champion of British fashion, and I don't think there's much disagreement here unless you're Cherie Booth – only joking Mrs Blair! – probably the hottest, coolest consort ever to live in Downing Street. Yes, I know, some of us have all the luck. But, call me naïve, I thought she might leave the political insights to me!

The idea, if memory serves, was for Sam, if she could

bear it, to tear out some cuttings and dash off some notes each week, to help with the memoirs a few years – or decades – down the line. Because, frankly, we're not all lucky enough to have an Alastair Campbell on the pay-roll, supplying volumes of detailed research notes, all at the big state's expense. No offence to Craig, but I think that's the kind of loyalty some of us can only dream of.

As this book testifies, Samantha's weekly record rapidly became much more ambitious, and one year on it seems I don't just get to sleep in the same, deliciously warm bed as Britain's yummiest mummy, most visionary stationery designer and most fearless fashion ambassa-dress, but with a genuine literary genius who happens to be called Samantha Cameron.

I'm no expert on diaries, but I know a man who is: step forward Michael Gove mega-brained educationalist and all round good egg. Govey informs me that I get to sleep – and occasionally, without going into details, a little more than that! – with the greatest diarist since James Boswell. And since most of us will be happy to take Govey's word on matters literary, I think I'd prefer to take his advice over that of the teaching unions; that Samantha's diary should be compulsory reading at Key Stage Four.

God knows it takes real powers of observation to bring some Coalition politicians to life – naming no names Vince Cable, you septic old fraud (only joking!) – and even the most dedicated public servant would have to admit that the daily grind of politics can be less than scintillating. Look at Europe. Foreign policy. House of Lords reform. Media ownership. Child poverty. Youth unemployment. Climate change. Scottish independence. Still with me? Indeed, and the list goes on and on.

Are these issues important? Absolutely 100 per cent no doubt about it, and political life would certainly be poorer without them, in fact some of us would never get to sleep. But do they create well-being? That's a different question. I certainly believe they can dominate the political land-scape to the detriment of the truly important issues: I'm talking well-being, happiness and even, dare I say it, that Big Society this government is working so hard – as I believe it has a responsibility to do – to build for our country. End of sermon!

Whatever nonsense you may have read about Anya's reaction, before she was given the Homeland Security brief, most friends and colleagues have not only recognised the portraits and events Samantha has so magnificently immortalised in these pages, but appreciated this picture of a genuinely happy little community where, with a little help from our friends, we have always found time to pause, laugh and, yes, I'm not ashamed to say it again – let sunshine win the day.

As for nicknames, although some people think them childish, we find that they lend our meetings an informal, very modern quality that only the totally humourless – no of course I'm not referring to you Edward Miliband, you adenoidal little squit (only joking!) – will fail to appreciate.

But it certainly helps if you have friends, like 'Honest' Phil Green, Julian 'Fishknife' Fellowes, George 'Oik' Osborne, Craig 'Whatever' Oliver, and Tommy 'the Fartmeister' Strathclyde – who has sportingly allowed Samantha to reveal the origin of his nickname. These, as Samantha's timeless pen portraits have proved, are people who can fill even the toughest, longest political day with banter, comradeship and, for those of us with a fully functioning sense of perspective, some utterly brilliant jokes. On which note, our joint thanks, as always, to Nick Clegg.

Enjoy.

David Cameron
August 2011

Samantha Cameron has insisted on an upgrade
to the Downing Street living quarters and
kitchen before moving in, it was revealed
yesterday ... When a neighbour once idly asked
Samantha about removal trucks taking them to
No. 10, she reportedly replied: 'I ****ing hope
not.'

Daily Mirror, 21 May 2010

Just back from a half-term break in Ibiza
with her children, Samantha Cameron
could compare tans with retail supremo Sir
Philip Green when they found themselves
thrown together at an awards ceremony.
Sam bumped into the Monaco-based
tycoon at the *Glamour* magazine bash in
London's Berkeley Square, where the
Tory leader's wife won the magazine's
accessories designer gong for her work as
creative director for upmarket stationery
company Smythson.

Daily Mail, 4 June 2010

'Going to keep a diary?' Dave said on coalition night. 'Cos I won't have time.' We were driving back from the Queen. Oh sure, I said, you know how much I love writing. Course I'm fucking not. Then he said, 'Absolutely sure?' and took this hideous object out of his briefcase, and I didn't have much choice, given it was one of my own, signature Wag-dazzlers, the medium-size manuscript book in fuchsia lambskin, and he'd sweetly got it customised with 'Mrs Cameron's Diary' in gold where it normally says 'Luncheons, Suppers and Dinners'. We couldn't talk any more, anyway, because his mobile went, and it was poor Cleggsy wanting to know what the Queen was like. 'Incredibly nervous,' Dave said. 'As you'd expect. But Sam soon put her at her ease.'

Then we looked at the Prime Minister's flat, which is basically a two-floor caravanette with a filthy carpet and walls the colour of sick. Hilarious. We were still going oh my actual God and taking photographs of each other doing vomit faces when the phone went. 'Very nice,' Dave told Cleggsy. 'Big. Loving the colours.'

Since then Dave's been in London thinking what to

cut, and I've been crying a lot in Ibiza, as any normal person would. I mean, a collapsing economy you can factor in. But who knew about Cherie's granite'n'pine kitchenette with wrought-iron handles, stained banquette seating and midget fridge? Plus the busy powder-blue carpets, louvred wardrobes, marble-topped commodes, nests of tables, pleated lampshades, lattice radiator-covers, glass-fronted bookshelves and floral pelmets? Got to hand it to the Blairs, I told Mummy, they knew how to make the average Bupa waiting room look like Versailles.

So round of applause for me getting back from Ibiza with a finished plan for a simple yet stylish family home: waxed cement floors, neutral tones, colour from the odd accented wall, sofas and – nod at tradition – a few vintage pieces. Once you knock through No. 10 into 11, the sightlines go right through from the open-plan kitchen to a glass wall overlooking Horseguards. I couldn't wait to show Dave. 'Surprise!' I said, when the children were asleep. And Dave went can it wait babes and looked around for his BlackBerry because it was vibrating somewhere, and even before he said wassup ma man, I knew it would be Nick.

Dealing with the deficit would affect 'our whole way of life' but not in a way that hits the vulnerable or 'divides the country', Mr Cameron said.

BBC News, 7 June 2010

David Cameron today welcomed Lady Thatcher to 10 Downing Street for a private meeting. The Prime Minister came to the door of No. 10 to welcome his predecessor and helped the visibly frail Thatcher from her limousine.

Guardian, 8 June 2010

Miriam González, who heads up the trade department of the international law firm DLA Piper, says that a political wife can be 'supportive without being submissive . . . I am sufficiently confident to understand I can have a proper career.'

Observer, 14 March 2010

Dave said to put in something about this historic speech he did saying our whole way of life would have to change, before he forgets. Actually it was amaze – I looked around while he was practising and thought God that is so true, soon all this will be totally unrecognisable. It already is, a little bit, since I hid everything except the bath under neutral throws from Mummy's. Makes it hard to find things though, I sat on a soft paleish object the other day when we had the Lib Dems in for drinks and it turned out to be Vince Cable, halfway under an ottoman. He said he was just checking the label and had we gone to Ipsa for guidance. God knows. Do they do throws?

The next thing, Cable was heading for the bathroom, Simon Hughes had found the swatches and I was like, help me Dave, but he was with Cleggsy in the bedroom, picking out ties. No sign of Miriam, of course, just in case anyone forgets how hard she works. So I asked Danny Alexander, who was so thrilled to be noticed, if he'd like to see how Nancy's rabbits are loving Sarah Brown's organic vegetable garden. All of her radishes disappeared in one day!

I thought there was no harm in asking – would he mind being incredibly kind and having them at weekends, obviously I'd make it worth his while? They hardly ever bite. So I ran back for cash, before Danny could change his mind, and was just going to ask David Laws if he thought twenty quid was too mean for two rabbit-sitting weekends a month if I threw in a leather key ring, when Cable was back in my face AGAIN, going why not just refresh the grouting, since it is only lightly stained? He says it nauseates him when people replace perfectly good bathroom fittings, even an unused bidet can be a handy place to refresh plants. And – get this, from a Lib Dem – we might not be here for long, anyway. All in that creepy uncle voice. I could easily have been in tears afterwards, but Dave was so adorable and said fuck the grouting, I'm the Prime Minister babes, you'll get your wet room, just give me time.

But I'm like, when? We're going backwards. Mrs T visited so it was throws off in case she got offended, even though all she said to me was 'Shouldn't you be at school?' Then throws back on again. Plus I have to get down to some proper work. It's just so hard to think luxury when you're living in squalor.

Britain and France's first ladies have apparently endured a tense day of pregnant pauses and strained exchanges together. While their husbands tried to project a united front amid global financial woes, Ms Bruni-Sarkozy and Mrs Cameron may need more time to find common ground.

Sky News, 18 June 2010

Carla Bruni-Sarkozy arrived in London this morning wearing a grey fitted dress by the British designer, John Galliano, couturier-in-residence at the house of Christian Dior … Samantha Cameron, who is remaining effortlessly chic during her pregnancy, struck an equally sombre note in a black-and-white, wool-crepe 'bra-bodice' dress by the London-based Emilia Wickstead.

Daily Telegraph, 18 June 2010

I was perfectly fine about it until people started going, 'Don't worry, obviously no one's looking, but what's the plan for Carla?', as if she was royalty rather than Mrs Nicolas Frankenstein, and I'd need a special ceremonial wardrobe. Of course old Cable poked his nose in, saying that if I needed to splash out, Mrs Cable swears by Florence and Fred at Tesco, some lovely things in the sale. Theresa May said she's no expert, but as the senior woman in cabinet, zebra print is always *très chic*.

The night before, Cleggsy texted, which was quite sweet I suppose: once with the French word for hello, then a reminder to make actual cheek contact in the air-kiss – how bizarro is that? – and finally to say he'd changed his mind about my outfit, how about that simple, faintly Colette-style frock I'd worn to the Queen's speech? He can be so transparent. I mean, I said to Dave, Miriam and the pathetic Cleggsy are well aware I was sitting next to Sarah Govey that day, not Helen of fucking Troy. Plus, last time I looked, I was the person who knew something about the fashion business. Dave said of course babes, and 'I wish you would call Nick Nick, but you always look lovely, go for bespoke English, remember the budget's coming.' So I wrote that down, specially, in case he forgets.

So I would totally blame him for what happened if the whole nightmare didn't make you wonder what the Foreign Office is actually for. I mean, Earth to William Hague, hello? Aren't there spies and stuff to warn us when some inexpertly embalmed alumnus of the Mick Jagger modelling academy is planning to make the Prime Minister's wife look like she shops mail-order, from Ukraine? Or worse. The very first thing she did, after the air kissing – in which she did NOT, nb Cleggsy, make skin contact – was to ask if the dress came from Florence and Fred. Then when we walked ahead of her, I could hear her whisper '*Regard Nicky – la marche des pingouins hahaha!*'

Over tea, she gave it everything – legs, hair, pelvis, and what Mummy says would definitely be considered semi-pornographic interest in my post-natal recovery, even for a famous *grande horizontale*. Dave says no-one has ever asked him before if '*éducation périnéale après l'accouchement*' is available on the NHS, and Carla cowishly made him admit he did not even know what it was. I mean, I said to Mummy, at least we know now how she hooks all her weird old men. But of course everybody does perineal education at yoga, so I just

9

went to Dave, 'Exercising the front bottom', before she could demonstrate, and for the first time all day Sarkozy looked really interested. 'It's supposed to restore the full quality of intimate relations after childbirth,' I said. 'Though some medics think it can increase elasticity at any time, *c'est pas vrai*, Carla?'

Babes, cd you check — does the cash look right? lusm.

Dear Danny, just the quickest of notes because we go off in five minutes — bless you for offering to do this, it is such a relief to know the rabbits will be in such amazingly safe and experienced hands! Dave says really not to worry <u>a bit</u> if you find you don't have time left over for the boxes because Vince is also going to be busy this weekend sourcing water-conserving sanitary ware, so sweet of him to offer, and George says he is fine about any coalition partners who are not yet able to work at his level! I wouldn't dream of bossing around an expert because you must have done this all the time at the ~~zoo~~ nature reserve! But could I <u>beg</u> you to make sure that the rabbits get their exercise — just a couple of times around St James's Park will be fine, Coulson says they only very rarely run off.

And a couple of boring little things, Churchill likes a bedtime book — non-fiction only — and Clemmie will only sleep on a bed — so this will be her first time with a Lib Dem!

And if you could clear the hutch <u>daily</u> you will earn many brownie points from a certain OCD sufferer! I enclose a twenty-pound note, as agreed, plus ten to spend on anything you like, you <u>must</u> — and don't hesitate to ring if you need, Perkins is always on duty between 6am and the shipping news.

Dave joins me in sending our literally undying gratitude,

Samantha.

PERFECT BABES —
RE CASH, ASK
COULSON WHAT
HE GOT THEN
HALF SHOULD DO
IT? LUSM.

Nick Clegg's wife has accepted a lucrative job with a major Spanish wind farm firm just weeks after her husband became Deputy Prime Minister.

Daily Mail, 10 June 2010

Nick Clegg was today forced to defend backing a rise in VAT as he faced a growing backlash from Liberal Democrats and saw his party fall in the polls.

Evening Standard, 24 June 2010

The package of budget measures is expected to be the most draconian in thirty years. The Chancellor will say that 'tough action' – raising taxes and cutting spending – is 'unavoidable' if the £155 billion deficit is to be brought under control.

Daily Telegraph, 22 June 2010

On her official website, Miss Bruni wrote: 'The companion of the new UK head of government is a kind of fashion icon. Aristocratic but bohemian, practitioner of yoga and close to the ecological cause.' And the tattoo, 'retained from her youth', is symbolic of 'a maverick style.'

Daily Mail, 28 June 2010

30 June 2010

God I hate newspapers. All those 'what the budget will mean for you' pieces, if you're old, unemployed or whatever, and Daddy says not one of them shows what Oik's plans mean for a struggling landowner in Scunthorpe and the effect on pig prices. And you just try being a typical high-net-worth mother struggling to survive in the luxury goods market, you literally don't exist.

I mean, will you still be allowed to spend your child benefit on a kitchen? Taps, specifically. I couldn't bother Dave, he was so deep into budgety stuff, then he had to go and swank around in Canada and he texted saying it was genius, a lot of really funny old guys but they loved him! But round here the drilling got so bad I didn't even know the doorbell had gone until Danny ran upstairs from exercising the hamster, since Nancy has inevitably lost interest, and said come quickly, and it's only little Cleggsy going 'Sorry, I know Dave's away.' He looked so totally lost and pathetic, even for him, that I was worried, plus Miriam was out, working her fingers to the bone flogging windfarms, as per.

So he was hunched on the sofa and I was like, oh no

hurry Nick, honestly, I'm only pregnant, abandoned in a fucking museum piece, trying to work, brainstorming names for this very simple austerity handbag I'm doing: nude, war-time lambskin, referencing gas-mask cases but not in an in-your-face kind of way. Actually I'm wondering about the Vince Bag, except he's so weird he'd be flattered. Anyway, finally Cleggsy confessed, tragic really, that the VAT thing is doing his head in, everyone's being so foul. So I explained why it will literally make no difference. As in, please – twenty quid more on a bag that costs £900? It just whets people's appetite. And if, very sadly, you can't afford a new bag, no worries. Literally the fairest tax on earth. Just before he left, all smiles again, he told me to check out Carla's website, she'd given me a nice mention.

'Nick wasn't being mean, babes,' Dave said, when I got through to his idiotic summit. And wasn't it nice to know Carla had called me a 'kind of fashion icon'? With my tattoo, 'retained from my youth'? Unlike the whole of her face then. And no, he said I couldn't send a few thank-you pizzas to the Elysée at 3am because of course the French delivery men would know she would never eat pizza. Which was good in a way, because, thinking about Carla, I realised I've never done enough using really ancient, distressed leather. So just as soon as they've finished the prototype, she's going to be the first owner of my first tribute accessory, kind of like the Kelly bag, but much more competitively priced: an über-luxe waste-facility in hand-stitched crocodile hide called the Carla Bin.

David Cameron has joined the likes of Winston Churchill, Barack Obama and Tony Blair in having his own wax statue at Madame Tussauds. The Prime Minister's likeness was unveiled by wife Samantha in a ceremony at the central London museum.

BBC News, 1 July 2010

Cornbury bridges the gap between traditional rock festival and an English garden fête ... It's the family-friendly, relaxed atmosphere that had the Prime Minister, David Cameron, who is the area's local MP, return for a fourth year with his family yesterday. The festival has been dubbed 'Poshstock' for its location on the 6,500-acre Cornbury estate owned by Lord and Lady Rotherwick, and for its clientele, who this year also included local Jeremy Clarkson.

Independent, 5 July 2010

My first solo outing! They'd finished this hysterical waxwork of Dave and when of course he made some lame excuse not to unveil it, because Hilto says you might as well choreograph a *Private Eye* cover, they said would I? So I'm like, sure, posing with a weird husband dolly on a boiling day when you're massively pregnant has got to be the dream gig, but Dave said oh, go on babes, they won't be horrible to you, got to start somewhere, plus if I go he can be too grand for waxworks without actually being rude. And all I'd have to do is smile at the waxwork and go 'amazing' – basically, just pretend to be Cleggsy. In fact, if I really didn't want to fill in, Nick had offered, so then, obvs, I was like, I'm in, no question.

And when I went outside and met wax Dave on the doorstep everyone was actually so sweet and I found myself saying loads of other random stuff, such as 'incredible' and 'they are such artists', which sort of reminded people I am a creative person in my own right. And I found I was suddenly quite keen on waxworks – until Cable turned up, waving his new B&Q seniors' card but actually wanting to know if 'that orange costume' was new, because he and Mrs C thought so, and did it really send out a helpful message just before Osborne's 40 per cent cuts threat? Unbelievable – since obviously the tangerine shift wasn't just new, but specifically chosen as a compliment to Cleggsy and the losers. You'd think all their jobs and the referendum on their votey thingy would shut them up, at least for a bit, but Dave says little touches still mean so much to them, specially now that I've decided not to call the austerity tote the Vince Bag. Whatever Nick says, I still don't think you can call a luxury handbag after a Liberal Democrat, even when you're channelling a depressiony, Jarrowy, rationingy sort of vibe.

Such a relief to get to the country, even though Hilto made us all go to Cornbury first, to underline that, underneath, Dave's much more Jackson Browne/Mumfords/trainers than Madame Tussauds/Rihanna/suits. But actually it was so worth it, with the children on merry-go-rounds and everyone toasting the budget, until there was the inevitable *Fawlty Towers* ringtone and Cleggsy's been thinking – again – wouldn't a proper working coalition have two waxworks? This time, I actually grabbed the phone.

'Loving the whole concept, Nick,' I said, 'but wait. Wouldn't it be sad if Miriam couldn't find the time to unveil it?'

> **Carole Caplin, a fashion and fitness adviser to Cherie Blair, was a guest at Chequers yesterday despite concerns over the alleged role of her lover – a convicted conman – in negotiating a property deal for the Prime Minister's family. Peter Foster, who has been jailed for fraud in Britain, the United States and his native Australia, claims to have acted for the Blairs in purchasing two flats in Bristol.**

Daily Telegraph, 2 December 2002

Tony Blair spent thousands of pounds of taxpayers' money entertaining a host of Britain's leading television celebrities at Chequers during his last fifteen months in power …

The guest list included Charlotte Church and Gavin Henson, and Tess Daly, the co-presenter of BBC1's *Strictly Come Dancing*, and her husband Vernon Kay, who is also a TV presenter. Other famous names included Lorraine Kelly and Fiona Phillips from *GMTV*, as well as Chris Evans, the BBC Radio 2 DJ. Richard Madeley dined with the Blairs. Steve McClaren, the England football manager, and his wife Kathryn, were also invited to Chequers, as was *Match of the Day 2* presenter Adrian Chiles.

Daily Telegraph, 26 July 2007

14 July 2010

Seriously loving Chequers. Even if it's unbelievably cramped if you want more than ten people to stay, and the pool's prehistoric. And the bathrooms are beyond disgusting, with scratchy tubs and Mrs T's turquoise net loo-roll tidies, and it's all got that kind of holiday rental feeling with Maeve Binchy novels and a games cupboard with KerPlunk ('please return to J Major', in Biro) and an old Monopoly board with the top hat missing. Plus the Go corner's all chewed – mice we assumed, then the housekeeper, Mrs Perkins (v sweet, completely understood about no first names), said 'Gordon' (!) gnawed it off one night after someone accidentally let him out. Regular occurrence, apparently.

In the end, Perkins says, it was Sarah (!) who asked if she wouldn't mind locking all the rooms at night; she was so worried about the historic collection, especially Cromwell's briefcase or whatever it is, but it was too late for Dorothy Macmillan's bloomers – completely shredded, although some people say she was just covering for Naomi Campbell.

So after Dave tipped Perkins (who will be a total treasure once she's over the Post-Traumatic Stress Disorder) to 'find' the keys, we had the most brilliant night going through cupboards which had literally not been opened for years. Govey, so brainy, practically screamed with excitement when we found an ancient visitors' book full of forgotten names. Like, in 2002, someone called Peter's written 'Ta muchly – call Carol if you wanna do biznis! XOXOXO' on a weekend when they also had 'Richard and Judy' – 'Left ya the Binchy, enjoy!!!!!' – and someone who's just left a smudged JP next to 'Will replace biccies, sorry about the trifle, be lucky'. Niall Ferguson will know.

Then we opened this creepy mahogany wardrobe and before Govey could stop us Dave had bagged Cherie's Burberry tote, Oik was in Tony's posing pouch and I'd just said 'one word, three syllables' (which was OMG – they'd never have got), when Dave accidentally dropped Cherie's hideous bag and out rolled this little compacty thing with lots of fluff stuck to it. So it was goodbye charades, unfort, but Govey said we should pause to consider a truly historic moment, apparently Andrew Roberts will be seething when he hears. And if it really does turn out to be

Cherie's missing contraceptive equipment, Dave says he knows the perfect place, next to Cromwell's briefcase, where Dorothy Macmillan's bloomers used to go.

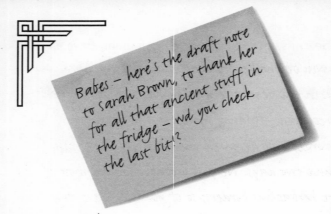

Babes – here's the draft note to Sarah Brown, to thank her for all that ancient stuff in the fridge – wd you check the last bit?

Dear Sarah,

How incredibly kind of you to leave the flat in such amazing shape, and with so many ~~interesting~~ delicious things to eat on our first night – it was actually the first time I had ever seen ~~a neep~~, neeps, sadly Dave and I had already eaten, but Pickles said they were ~~indescribable~~ indescribably delicious! I am so impressed by your ~~in your face puritanism~~ obvious aversion to waste – if only more people were like that! And Pickles is also a great fan of ~~mould~~ mature bananas so they disappeared in no time, along with that little saucer of – I'm not sure, there was cling film over it – ~~grouting~~ semolina? I know you will be thrilled to hear that all your hard work in the vegetable garden has also been much appreciated — Nancy's rabbits, Churchill and Clemmie, had devoured the whole thing within around two days. We will probably return most of it to herbaceous borders, so if you ever have any spare veg north of the border, you know where to send it!

Anyway I have been doing the Chequers inventory with the housekeeper — boring! — and thought I should confirm with you that there was just the plastic tableware when you arrived — and no tumblers or wine glasses, or crockery, or vases, or mirrors or breakables of any description? Of course, with small children I can totally see how amazingly practical that is, but Perkins insists there used to be crystal glasses and dinner services and a few charming yet fragile decorative items before 2007, even after Mrs Blair had a big clear out. It's old-fashioned of me, I know, but I suppose

more traditional stuff comes in handy on formal
occasions! And it would be quite tedious to have to
buy replacements, or use our own, if by chance,
the originals had ~~just been smashed by Gordon~~
~~unhappily met a series of accidents~~ just been put
out of harm's way.

Oh, and the same of course applies to the phones
and smaller occasional tables. It's a shame about
that large marble Louis XVIII credenza,
apparently the crack is irreparable.

Do let me know — a tweet would do! — when you
get the chance.

All our best wishes for your new life in ~~hell~~
Kirkcaldy,

samantha

Asked by ITV's Mary Nightingale if she was willing to 'go out and hit the campaign trail, like Samantha Cameron?' Mrs Clegg, a lawyer, said: 'Well, listen, I don't have the luxury of having a job that I can simply abandon for five weeks, and I imagine that that is the situation for most people in the country.'

Daily Telegraph, 20 March 2010

Wearing a burka can be 'empowering' and 'dignified' for Muslim women, one of the Government's most senior female ministers has said. The controversial remarks by Caroline Spelman, who as Environment Secretary is the second most powerful woman in the Cabinet, were immediately described as 'moronic' and 'bizarre'.

Daily Telegraph, 18 July 2010

David Cameron will travel to Washington today for his first official visit to the United States since becoming Prime Minister in May.

Evening Standard, 19 July 2010

21 July 2010

Who knew diplomacy was so tiring? Dave's loving it, but
it's not exactly shattering for him handing out all the
presents that I picked with Bells, plus they've got
ambassadors to argue about all the things like BP, so
sad for the fishes Danny says, although tbh I slightly
feel, not being a fish person, plenty more where they
came from. Anyway I was totally on my own in the flat,
unless you count Danny, catching flies for Nancy's new
gecko, when this sinister recycled envelope arrived and
I knew – you can so always tell from the stationery – it
had to be Miriam.

'Dear Sam' (bit familiar after the way she's made me
out to be some fucking princess), 'Now that your
refusal to travel to America demonstrates a
commendable determination to be seen as a powerful
and vibrant woman in your own right, I feel it is time
we met. Please join us for tortillas and some
emancipated literary chat. *The Golden Notebook* is on
its way. *Saludos*.' Excuse me, how mean can you get, I
said to Danny, plus the amazing nerve of it, she knows
perfectly well luxe stationery is my territory, I mean as
if I would start banging on about EU company law –

but he said no, I'd love it, Sarah Teather says it changed her life.

I was about to say forget it, end of, when, ping, there's a panicky text from Dave going please babes, do it for the special relationship, go for something hippy/unthreatening – maybe the maxi dress from Ibiza? So Monday night, instead of hanging the Banksys, a surprise for when he's back, I'm en route to Penge or wherever with a scented candle, and of course I haven't done the wretched homework because this book is literally fifteen times the size of a big Jilly Cooper, so I'm frantically calling Hunty who puts me on to Theresa who passes me to Caroline, who says she's sure Lessing's *haram*, ending up with Picklesy, who's still warning me off tortilla unless it's been very thoroughly cooked, when we park outside this quite darling little cottage, and there's Cleggsy in the garden, pegging up nappies. Miriam says she never lets him disturb the book talk.

So in the kitchen (rough sycamore worktops, Amish-ish units, no island) there's a heap of literally the saddest, most über-feminist handbags I have ever seen. Plus around fifteen matching owners glowering over the tortillas. But thank heavens for Pickles, because nobody disagrees when I say that in Anna Wulf, Lessing goes to the heart of the progressive woman's dilemma: how many of us can reconcile our disparate selves, shouldn't a women's book group be talking investment bags as well as ideas? Whatever, everyone except Miriam wants a discount and I've finally got a name for my austerity tote: the Doris.

The cabinet met at Chequers yesterday for its first full political session, without civil servants, since the Coalition was formed. There in the leafy Buckinghamshire countryside, far from the hustle and bustle of Whitehall, they took stock of the challenges that lie ahead.

Independent, 24 July 2010

Perkins went so utterly postal when she heard we'd be around seventeen for the weekend that I slightly wanted to cry, since no wives or children were involved, and hardly any beagles, but Dave said be cool babes, remember Gordon was a loner, give her time. Then Mummy said absolutely not, rule one with staff is never let them brood, remember Simms when you were small and the poor rabbits? Such good advice because it turned out, hilarious really, to be all about that vomit by the pool and as soon as we'd fixed a price for accidents (£20, or £30 on Sundays, bargain!) Perkins was fine. But sad, really, because she is fascinating on the history of the place, if only Govey had bunged her a tenner after the accident, instead of *The Life and Times of Siegmund Warburg*, they would have so got on, but then you think of his background, can't be helped.

Everyone was fairly tense when the coach arrived, but after several Bloody Marys the PowerPoints flew past, at least until Govey's Europe lecture, which sadly crashed some time around the Napoleonic Wars. Perkins said sorry, typical Chequers electrics, but Dave quickly went no worries awaydayers, I think we all know about the Charge of the Light Brigade! So after lunch they could choose between beagling, table-tennis or rolling down a hill in a Portaloo, and I could see the poor Liberals looking so conflicted even though Oik was paying for any damage, then at dinner Dave said Huhne had managed seven complete revolutions before the toilet exploded; I mean, who knew?

It was a bit tricky later, asking the girls if they wouldn't be more comfortable moving next door while the men had their port, but once Caroline – or Khalida, whatever she calls herself now – had said purdah is so empowering Theresa could hardly stay on her own, and afterwards it really was the most intense bonding experience Dave says, except for Cable sulking all through, and when I drifted off they were still singing 'We Are the Coalition' outside the police hut. Doubling up just brought them closer, except for Cable, and I hardly noticed Cleggsy – or no more, I told him, than you would a large dog. Perkins was so thrilled with her £120 bonus and I know, once she's done the clean-up, Cable's trousers will turn up somewhere.

David Cameron has begun a two-day visit to India with the aim of strengthening relations and creating jobs in the UK. He has also used the visit to speak about the relationship between India and Pakistan. He said, 'We have to make sure that the Pakistan authorities are not looking two ways, they must only look one way.'

BBC News, 28 July 2011

What to get the world's most powerful couple is a dilemma to tax even Samantha Cameron, who works in the world of luxury gifts.

And Mrs Cameron's choice of present for Barack and Michelle Obama – presented by her husband on his first visit to the White House as Prime Minister – raised eyebrows.

Though Mrs Cameron, who is just weeks away from giving birth to her fourth child, has not been able to make the trip to the US, aides said she had selected a £2,500 painting by a former 'street' artist repeatedly arrested for criminal damage.

Daily Mail, 21 July 2010

Shortly after being elected MP for Surrey Heath in 2005, Mr Gove furnished a house in north Kensington, west London, for which he claimed the Additional Costs Allowance.

Over a five-month period between December 2005, and April 2006, he spent more than £7,000 on the semi-detached house, which Mr Gove, 41, and his wife Sarah Vine, a journalist, bought for £430,000 in 2002. Around a third of the money was spent at Oka, an upmarket interior design company established by Lady Annabel Astor, Mr Cameron's mother-in-law.

Mr Gove bought a £331 Chinon armchair from there, as well as a Manchu cabinet for £493 and a pair of elephant lamps for £134.50. He also claimed for a £750 Loire table, a birch Camargue chair worth £432 and a birdcage coffee table for £238.50.

Daily Telegraph, 11 May 2009

4 August 2010

So before Dave went to India, he said why not pick some
art for the flat, supposing it ever gets finished, which is
so kind of the government to offer but quite disturbing
really, because it means Gordon Brown must have
personally chosen that flayed lion being eaten by rats, in
actual skin, that used to hang over the bed. But it was
thanks but no thanks, I told Mummy, because you'd
think from the list there hadn't been an important artist
since Sergeant and, to be honest, everyone's got one of
those. I mean, hello, Government Art Collection – Banksy
or Eine, anyone? It's as if the whole avant-garde street-
arty thing never happened, and God knows what you're
meant to do if you're going for a pared-down look with
basically an eclectic mix of bold abstracts, photographs
and irreverent stencils to subvert the hideous corporate
vibe – losing battle, admittedly, with Cherie's crystal
pelmets, the architect says she actually got them listed.

The little clerk in charge was so sweet at first,
apparently Cherie hasn't returned the Sergeants yet
anyway, but he was sure there was a Vanessa Bell
somewhere, lots of orange, some lovely greens, very
modern, 'look lovely with your futons'. Well, I went,

absolutely no disrespect but if this is really all you've got, would the government like to borrow some things of ours, since there's way too much big stuff for the flat?

I can't be certain until they've repainted the drawing room in Blighted Udder, as intended – unbelievable Cable really thought I'd be taken in by the Homebase magnolia – but we could probably spare the large Gobshite and a couple of quite rare Philths, from when he was still using his own bodily fluids. And instead of leaping at the chance, the clerky man actually went all huffy, and I was like, I do have a degree in fine art, for what it's worth, as well as counting Gobshite, Dregz and the Grotmeister as personal friends.

Then I texted Dave who said some people are born chippy, look at Pakistan, and forget the big state babes, just ring Govey if you want to offload some of the mistakes. Which was such a brilliant idea because they really haven't got a thing unless you count those Anglesey seascapes from John Lewis Online. They must dream of living with a genuine Tosspot.

Dear Mrs Blair,

Thank you so much for your note — what a lovely
picture of you and Mr Blair in front of your new
cabin cruiser! — and its very kind wishes. Dave
and I were also terribly touched by the gift of
your memoirs — although of course the flat
already tells its own story of your time in
Downing Street, I think of you each time I go into
the old kitchen and see all that dark granite and
the rustique handles! I often wonder where you got
the idea. And I think it is so sensible of you to ask
what is going to happen to 'your' units which will
indeed have to go as part of our refurbishment.
I hope you are not offended, believe me I have

<u>begged</u> the architect to keep them, but he is a total authoritarian and simply insisted on his own 'look'! So do let me know when would suit and we can have the skip driven directly to you, instead of the dump — which property were you thinking of?

On a more literary note, how kind of you to ask for an interview, so you can update <u>The Goldfish Bowl</u>. I look forward to reading it — and really don't worry about sending one, there are still around thirty copies in the Chequers library. But I am afraid Dave is making me write my own diary of our time here and I get the feeling he is rather proprietorial about it! So I am afraid the answer will have to be no, at risk of missing out on your kind offer of a discount when the next edition comes out!

While I am writing, could you possibly let me know what to do with some of the odds and ends which have turned up at Chequers? Without being too explicit, you seem to have forgotten a small piece of medical equipment — would you like it sent on?

Then, in our bathroom cupboard, there is that quite large collection of complimentary-size soaps, bath-hats, shampoos, sewing-kits, miniature jams, sugar sachets, disposable slippers etc from your travels around the world — please let me know if they are of any sentimental interest.

Finally, I am sure I am being completely stupid — and Perkins, being the soul of discretion, simply will not say — but is it true that a large Landseer used to hang in the hall, over the fireplace? Sarah Brown says the gap was there when they arrived. And a pair of Sergeants seem to be missing from the dining room. They are such ghastly, old-fashioned painters, I know, and how easily these things can get accidentally removed in the haste of packing. But do let me know if you can provide any clues!

Very best wishes

Samantha Cameron

The Prime Minister is travelling to Cornwall today for a 'PM Direct' meeting with up to 50 local people at a school. Downing Street suggested that these meetings will be held at regular intervals through the year.

Daily Telegraph, 9 July 2010

Aristocratic David Cameron yesterday claimed he was just an ordinary member of Britain's middle-class. In a question-and-answer session in Manchester, the Old Etonian said there was a problem with Sure Start children's centres because middle-class parents like my wife and me got all the services.

Daily Mirror, 11 August 2010

Prime Minister David Cameron and Pakistan's President Asif Ali Zardari are meeting for an informal dinner amid continuing diplomatic tensions. Officials hope the strain caused by Mr Cameron's recent comments – that elements in Pakistan were promoting terrorism – will begin to ease.

BBC News, 5 August 2010

Dave said we must keep on sharing the pain, big time, and could I think of anything fresh for the 'PM Direct' gig, which is hard because we've done all the big money-saving things like not wearing hats or having proper holidays and me wearing one sad old frock after another, and honestly you'd imagine having Mr Zardari all weekend was enough pain-sharing for anyone, thank you very much, for around three million years. Though he did cheer up when I told him he still had time to make the Selfridges sale on Sunday, which was a nice way for him to show he was feeling the pain as well, what with the dreadful floods.

But Dave says Hilto says absolutely no serious shopping for us before the comprehensive spending review, which is the tiniest bit unfair, I told Mummy, because no one looks at Miriam and counts up what she spends on all her funny shirts and cardies, especially as they never see her. And look at Hilto, sweating and disgustingness is kind of his look but I do actually have to think a bit fashion forward, plus minimal doesn't mean cheap. And Mummy said do try La Redoute, people swear by the lingerie, and I would so do that except how do you let the public know what you're sacrificing in well-fitting bras? It is like when Perkins said why don't we use up all the Bronco the Browns left behind, you can't swank about hard toilet paper. I mean old Cable is so clever with his Gandhi act, never off the tube with his ancient old briefcase, even though, for all anyone knew, it could be literally stuffed with millions of pounds worth of things from Selfridges or Agent Provocateur.

So while Dave was saying that council flats can't be for ever, which is terribly sad for people leaving a custom-made island and brushed-steel splashbacks they've probably paid for themselves, I was checking out every money-saving tip on earth except for Primark, because Cleggsy still draws the line at child labour though Dave says give him time. Texted him to say sorry babes we are already cut to the total bone, just wish you could say how hard we are trying to be properly ordinary, and he texted straight back 'how brilliant R u babes watch and learn'. So his speech was actually brilliant and Hilto thinks some people will definitely have believed it, and now everyone knows we're just as middle class as the poor I think the Bronco could go to the Cables, shame to waste it.

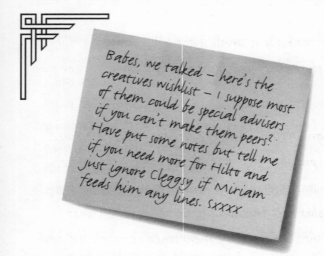

Babes, we talked — here's the creatives wishlist — I suppose most of them could be special advisers if you can't make them peers? Have put some notes but tell me if you need more for Hilto and just ignore Cleggsy if Miriam feeds him any lines. Sxxxx

International Trade Envoy — Anya Hindmarch — obvs already marv on party fundraising, accessories etc but also SO idealistic — Hilto has her I'm Not a Plastic Bag.

International Trade Envoy 2 — Tamara Mellon. You remember when you and Govey practically went mad over a picture of a naked woman plus cat? Well, her. Is also utter business genius. Does Jimmy Choos. Plus, basically, my life will not be worth living if you ask Anya and not her!

Prisons — Cath Kidston. Not sure of her politics, but there is literally nothing she does not know about making a small space look comfy, totally owns that cluttered, vintage, suburban-austerity vibe.

Foreign Office — Johnnie Boden. You know your black polo shirts? Well they all come from there, ditto swimmers. Total genius and so incredibly nice plus does this special 25 per cent Cabinet discount. Sarah Govey mentioned it when she had to return her 'sassy beach kaftan', after the beads made her nearly drown, and he said fine, plus peerage would obvs win Mumsnet points.

Treasury — Mary Portas. Mary Queen of Shops on the telly, channelling this kind of amaze, dominatrixy thing? Her. Business genius. Could easily control Oik. Lesbian aristocracy.

Social Mobility Tsar — Julian Fellowes. I know, insanely snobbish but has biggie for ITV coming up plus Mummy says knows EVERYTHING about class, servants, etc. Also says he would absolutely have to have peerage as research tool.

Health – Kirsty Allsopp. Says she's done housing, got the t-shirt, wants new challenge. Obvs terrifyingly efficient so, kind of, what is not to like, NHS-wise?

British fashion/style ambassador – Niall Ferguson, now based in NY. You know from telly, history etc but some people think is also quite hot, plus travels, exotic girlfriend – brilliant for upscale British accessories?

Fixing Broken Britain – is this one for Colin and Livia Firth? Both very caring.

Blue Skies Thinking – Honest Phil. Obvs already v busy, but could do so much more to combat waste, eg he says Audit Commission is total waste of space.

Arts/BBC – Sadie Frost? Incredibly creative, acted before she went into fashion/lingerie. Ex, Jude Law is in The Talented Mr Ripley, the one who wasn't Matt Damon? – knows literally everyone in Primrose Hill so could keep eye on Miliband — how perfect is that?

Big Society — Banksy. I know, terribly anti-establishment, but Brangelina, Keanu etc all have, so basically completely SWEET (plus the Hiltos have the rat print in their downstairs loo) — brilliant for getting charities on side, Philip Blond to mentor?

Fighting the Premature Sexualisation of Young Girls Tsar — Nadine keen to do, but is she hot enough? Ask the Fartmeister?

Minister without Portfolio — Carol Vorderman.

Manufacturing — Helena Bonham Carter. Makes a lot of her own clothes.

Education — Kate Moss. Even Hilto would know! so iconic and a role model and also a tiny bit common, in a really sweet way, so would def help fight obesity in schools.

High Speed Rail link — Tracey Emin. Desperate to be involved. (Plus, we are still hoping for that neon piece.)

Communities — Dylan Jones. You promised you would do something for him. Don't worry — I think he would def turn down. Or just get Anya to call a bag after him?

Europe Special Envoy — John Galliano. This will be news to Hilto but he runs Dior in Paris, so über-European and is basically the most genius, on-trend creative currently working in fashion, anywhere in the whole world, even Anna Wintour thinks he is <u>God</u>.

> Sir Philip Green has been forced to defend his appointment as a government spending adviser amid claims that his wife is a tax exile. The billionaire retailer has been recruited by David Cameron to lead a review scrutinising the past three years in order to identify waste.

Daily Mail, 13 August 2010

> **David Cameron has made time for an interview with the *Sun* marking the coalition's first 100 days. He has used this interview to point out that he learned from Margaret Thatcher and New Labour to move fast as a government and take big decisions early on.**

Guardian Politics blog, 18 August 2010

18 August 2010

Yay! I can hardly believe it's 100 days, which is only *frowns, counts fingers* five leg-waxes or three haircuts, slightly more I suppose if you have highlights, and yet so much has happened, even things they said were impossible like the new log basket arriving from Romania *faints*.

Dave said why not try those descriptive thingies people do on Twitter because if my diaries are read in future *blushes* he thinks they will really bring the writing *holds pen* to life. Really *weeps with relief* it is only snagging stuff now, in the flat, though we'll have to replace the rug *cross face* where Sir Philip was so ill after the fight, but Dave said chill babes, you can't pass a political milestone like this without a celebration and he's probably never played a proper drinking game before, are they even legal in Monaco?

And until all the fuss, everyone was loving Honest Phil's Topshop To Go discount party rail, typical Huhne to kick up a stink about a mistake over his change, and of course Phil would have immediately made up the difference if he hadn't been distracted by that silly argument after the last game of Find the Lady. Oik's still upset, but I know he heard worse than 'get me another drink, you fucking tosser' at Oxford if not with the Deripaskas, although I suppose they say it in Russian.

But I am a bit worried *worried face* because Philip is Dave's first big fashion appointment, and if he can't fit in with the other boys God knows how they'll take to Johnnie Boden at the Foreign Office. Then I'd pencilled in Sadie Frost for the BBC cuts and Kate Moss for education. Because Kate is in her understated way such a hard worker with a total horror of waste, she says you could save millions by making one school dinner feed three, plus the children would look and feel fabulous.

The rag trade is actually full of amazing thinkers, look at the Prada gel bag, so it's terribly unfair, I said to *crosses self* Cable, when he started playing up about Phil, to hold zero political experience against them. I mean, 100 days ago Oik could barely count and now look, so before you rubbish Honest Phil ask yourself what you know about Topshop.

David Cameron has said he is a 'very proud dad' after his wife Samantha gave birth to a girl, their fourth child. The baby – weighing 6lb 1oz – was delivered by caesarean section while the family was on holiday in Cornwall.

BBC News, 24 August 2010

Millionaire David Rowland quit as Tory treasurer yesterday after a rebellion by Conservative donors at damaging revelations about his business affairs. In a grave embarrassment for David Cameron, the property tycoon once branded 'a shady financier' in Parliament, jumped ship after disclosures about his high living and aggressive business tactics.

Daily Mail, 20 August 2010

If the AV referendum is lost, then Clegg will have a very difficult time keeping his party united and in the coalition. But if Clegg makes clear how much AV means to his party, then the chances of it being defeated increases as Labour voters and those dissatisfied with the coalition see it as a chance to bring it down.

Spectator, 21 August 2010

Florence Rose Endellion's third name refers to a village near where the PM and his wife have been holidaying.

Independent, 25 August 2010

Shattered and literally mental from no sleep, but Dave says it's vital we get the diary going again before stuff starts happening. So I said well why don't you bloody well write it and he said if anything he's more wrecked than I am since he's the one who has to actually get up while I can 'just doze off again'. Lolz.

I mean nobody could sleep through those howls, Mummy says she's never heard anything like it albeit she generally used to sleep in the next county when we were small, and God knows how we're going to cope in the council flat when there's not even a cupboard for the doula. After nine million broken nights I'm like, enough, bring on the controlled crying, but Dave goes come on babes, Cleggsy's used to being comforted after just a couple of rings, do you want to traumatise him just before the comprehensive spending review? So we were going to cut out the 4am call but the first night the poor boy was in floods about his votey thing, and now Dave says to put off starting the routine until he's properly back at work, which probably means never.

Am heroically, in the circs, halfway through thank yous for Philip Florence, though Dave says we may as well just start calling her Florence, since she's never going to answer to Philip, but we won't tell Uncle Phil yet because of all her presents his Learjet really is sooo our favourite, even if Hilto insists we can't personally keep, it came in this amazing matching hangar, pure fabulousness although, tbh, the white leather seats could be more on trend. Actually, not to be ungrateful, but most of the stuff from Dave's rich-listers is just begging to be re-homed – equestrian bronze of Spotty Rowland anyone? – and God knows if Oxfam will take that set of Filipina slaves from some random Russian, even in the Knightsbridge branch. Mummy sweetly offered to get the gold tanning unit melted down, except, hideously embarrassing, I've forgotten exactly which of the noovs it came from – probably a hedge fund manager if it wasn't Simon Cowell, or was he the erotic jade fishknives? – and Hilto says to be very careful, we mustn't upset our new best friends.

FLORENCE THANK YOUS

Daddy — field outside Goole, plus sty and two pregnant sows (plus some money)

Mummy — two per cent discount on the bookshelves and glasses (until Jan '11)

Bob Diamond — money

Andy — satellite baby-listening device

Anya — week's internship in summer 2028. Money.

Peter Stringfellow — babygro with 'Future Porn Star' on front, money

Spotty Rowland — money

Ed Vaizey — Nursery Rhymes on Kindle

Rebekah – Chumpneys new mummy's luxe pampering w/e, positive <u>sun</u> editorial

Michael Ashcroft – money

Danny Alexander – pet adder

Oik – money

Tamara – My First Uggs. Money.

Tracey – used-tampon musical mobile, plays 'Baa Baa Black Sheep' (insure)

Vince Cable – one box recycled swaddling bands

Govey and Sarah – <u>The Absolutely Splendid Bumper Vintage Book for Babies</u>

Eric Pickles – Terry's Chocolate Orange.

The Cleggsys – piggy bank

Andy Coulson, the No. 10 communications chief, found himself in the direct line of fire in the *News of the World* phone-hacking scandal tonight when a former colleague alleged that he issued direct orders to journalists to carry out the illegal practice.

Guardian, 3 September 2010

Victoria Beckham to branch into BAGS!
And now it's been confirmed! The range of handbags is currently in development, with Hillier, one of the best in the biz, on board in the role of consultant.

Grazia, 6 August 2010

15 September 2010

Politics is so full of surprises – who knew that Andy Coulson would turn out to be totally psychic? Every time the phone goes these days it's Andy, which is 1) kind of irritating in Fashion Week, God knows how he got my number, and 2) strange, since he always knows what I'm doing, even when that's literally impossible. Like, I'm on the way out, the phone goes and he'll say loving the dress, oh are you off out, pity about the traffic, I left you my *Sun* in the car, all the latest on the Rooneys, unless I'd prefer the *Times*, plus there's a Sky brochure featuring some great bundles, did I know Sky Multiroom is the perfect way to keep the whole family entertained?

Quite sweet, I suppose, but like I texted Mummy, it really creeps me out, then suddenly there's a ping, and I'm like oh my actual God because it's a text from Andy saying he knows he can seem quite creepy, no one hates his creepiness more than he does, but he's actually burdened with this gift thingy which means he hears all and sees all. And before I can go excuse me Mr Weird, I meant creepy as in promoting Sky bundles in Downing Street, he says, seriously, his inner eye can see an unbelievably famous actress – Sienna Miller it looks like – in the Bond Street shop, right now, buying a fashion diary and a small pink notebook with Whatever on the front. So I phoned the shop and it's all true, except she changed her mind at the last minute and picked a Yes We Can! notebook, but still in pink, which is unbelievable.

So when I asked Dave, he said of course babes, paranormal powers are the whole point of Andy, like the oracle at Delphi, but his gift really freaks some people out so we try to keep it quiet. No offence, I said to Andy, when he called ten seconds later, but I don't see why you couldn't do that from Delphi. Or at least, Basildon, I think he's from Basildon. And if he's going to virtually live here, he could at least prophesy for everyone. It would really have helped to know that Victoria Beckham is doing a signature tote.

It seems the Deputy PM's wife has been keeping her passion for fashion under wraps – until now – as today she launched a new ethical fashion range. The mother-of-three posed for pictures at an event to promote the label this morning. The trade lawyer looked chic in an emerald green dress by David Szeto with a white Zadig & Voltaire blazer.

Daily Mail, 16 September 2010

David Cameron today drew parallels between the Pope's teachings and his own vision of a 'Big Society'. Speaking at the end of the pontiff's state visit, the Prime Minister described the past four days as 'incredibly moving'.

Sun, 20 September 2010

So instead of being all peaceful with the Lib Dems away it has been quite difficult because, like Andy foretold, the Pope had to choose the exact same week to come and fight the forces of secularism. But I wonder about Andy's paranormal powers, because when Miriam suddenly reared up in colour-block green and her mother's old shoes – slightly eeuw, no? – raving about recycling, and I went why didn't you warn me, he said well there is still free will plus I've checked, not a dicky bird on Clegg's phone. I mean, I just do not know what Dave sees in him. Because if he really heard and saw all he wouldn't have gone: by the way, what's the plan for conference, something from M&S that showed off my shapely pins, he'd bet, or his name wasn't Andy 'the scrote the Tories trust' Coulson, would I let him know? Actually, I haven't got a clue after Miriam's look-at-me number, geniusly disguised as an I'm-too-brainy-to-shop-eco routine. Incredible, really, when she knows I'm in the luxury business. To be honest, I said to Dave, I could easily start wearing cardigans and condemning vacuous green posturing – except, as a national fashion ambassador, I haven't got time to worry about tragic legal workaholics. You just think: what next, a march against handbags led by Miriam and Vince? A bonfire of pink stuff in Parliament Square? But Dave said no way will that happen babes, he'll legislate first.

It is a good thing I'm quite secular, actually, because a spiritual person might be shocked by that sort of attention seeking, especially in pope week, which went brilliantly, Dave said, and really showed – NB Miriam Clegg – that faith is part of the national conversation. For example, I was conversing with Mummy when she said Holy Christ had I seen the state of Archbishop's House in the photos, think Claridge's Powder Room minus the gratuities saucer, she just longed to do the makeover, classy but nothing *über*-luxe, how long was the Pope staying because she could get an Oka catalogue biked round pronto with a complimentary armorial bin, perfect for the Vatican. So I asked Andy, but something told him the Pope had already left.

ED MILIBAND WINS LABOUR LEADERSHIP RACE

Ed Miliband, at the age of forty the younger of the two brothers, presented himself as the 'change' candidate who would end the New Labour era of Tony Blair and Gordon Brown.

Daily Telegraph, 25 September 2010

'I relish the chance to take on David Cameron. We may be of a similar age, but in my values and ideals I am of a different and new generation. The new generation is not simply defined by age, but by attitudes and ideals.'

Ed Miliband, 28 September 2010

It was not just Ed Miliband's big day yesterday. As he took on the leadership mantle, Justine was transformed by a quietly effective makeover. Thank God! This was a far cry from her appearance during the leadership campaign in London. Back then, Mr and Mrs Awkwardly-Earnest looked like a pair of geeks who had just signed up for a Scientology course. Justine appeared to have dressed herself from a North London charity shop.

Daily Mail, 26 September 2010

I was rather loving Igglepiggle or whatever, the new Labour boy who looks just exactly like a thumb, because honestly I said to Mummy, are not his ears literally to die for, until Dave went, seriously, wait up babes, let's see what he has to say to the squeezed middle, which is what everyone calls people who can't afford Spanx. But when I watched little Fred – Ed? Ted? – whatever, goggling away at his little conference it was sweetly lol hilarious. I was like, forget politics, he would still make the most brilliant soft toy: wiggly ears, googly eyes and a tuft of hair and Mr Thumby could retail for at least £9.99, perfect stocking-filler, Mummy is already costing the felt.

Perhaps Dave's right, though, because, underneath, Mr Thumby turned out to be really quite sinister, I mean even the children know it is rude to go on about people's ages, and he was so mean to his brother which is also inappropriate in a lovable soft toy. And anyway his maths must be useless because if he likes young people well excuse me, he ought to like the coalition because a three-year difference isn't enough to make Dave 'old generation' and being thirty-nine I am actually a year younger than him! Or am I missing something?

Danny, who is so clever with figures and animals, says that Thumby thinks Tory years are like dog ones, like Daddy's black labrador actually being 98, which is why he told Dave 'we may be of a similar age but I am of a new generation'. So I'm like fine, if we're going to be brutally frank has anyone bothered to tell Ms Justine Thornton, aged 40? I don't think so, tbh. Otherwise why would she be channelling Shirley Williams?

Not to be unkind, but the cardy over a frock thing can be a kind of cute, pulled-together look like Nigella, or it can be so tragic that you want to scream 'lose the mismatched shopper and scuffed shoes, get a blow dry, think minimal, no heels below four inches, forget Topshop and if you do nothing else, do not show your old-generation Labour legs in a knee-length dress made of old bath hats, Cherie's been there and done that'. But I think it's probably too late. Justine and I are of a similar age (ish) but, philosophically and taste-wise, I am of a new generation.

Dave — is this what Hilto wanted? I think they would all help unless it's easier to just do U-turn on child benefit??? Lusm.

SOME IDEAS FOR MAKING MUMSNET LIKE DAVE AGAIN.

The expression 'yummy mummy' prohibited as hate speech.

Designate all parking within a quarter of a mile of a John Lewis as (free) mother-and-baby. Prison sentences for non-parents using these places.

Non-parents (except waitresses) to be banned from Carluccios, at all times.

Govt commission to investigate legislating on inappropriate children's clothing & punitive deterrents for suppliers — Nadine Dorries to head?

Windfall tax on Space NK.

All pavements to be re-designated buggy-only highways (plus appropriate fines).

The right to give birth anywhere, eg on mountainside, in river etc, with minimum four midwives in attendance.

Mothers who put under-tens in high heels to be re-educated or have children taken into care.

All working mothers of under-25s to have the right to first choice of holidays.

Silver Birkenstocks taken out of tax.

Elderly to give way to mothers on buses.

Classification system, as in films, for scary shop windows at Hallowe'en.

Revise licensing rules to ban individuals without accompanying children from gastropubs on

Saturdays and Sundays, between hours of 11.30am and 8pm.

NHS Pilates classes — parents only.

CBeebies to be run 24/7 as condition of licence fee.

Tate Modern to be redesignated children's play area, to stop families being bothered by unaccompanied adults.

PERFECT BABES —
GO WITH THE
DORRIES
COMMISSION TO
START?

Child benefit payments for all higher-rate taxpayers will be stopped to pay for wider welfare reform and to show that 'we are all in this together', George Osborne said today.

Guardian, 4 October 2010

The joy on the Prime Minister's face was easy to read on Wednesday as he was reunited with Samantha and little Florence, picking them up from Birmingham train station. Gazing at her husband as he held their little girl, Samantha looked equally happy to be back at his side. The thirty-nine-year-old was bang on trend in a camel-hued coat paired with a white shirt and dark jeans.

Hello, 6 October 2010

Total. Fucking. Nightmare. Because I said to Dave what exactly is the point of spending literally years of your life sucking up to Mumsnet if the first big thing you do makes them all go mental and actually who can blame them? I mean what next, a yoga tax? Ugg rationing? VAT on me-time? He was like, tell me about it babes from now on you rule, so sweet, but I'm still waiting for a call from Oik so I can say I hate to say I told you so.

And he can't wriggle out of it because I've still got the envelope from that night at Chequers with the Scrabble scores on one side and, on the back, the sums where he proved that scrapping child benefit was a no-brainer, everyone was doing high fives and going Oik you legend; it really did not help they were all wasted.

So I waited until breakfast before going excuse me do you realise what this could do to luxury leather goods? Not to mention Fitflops, aromatherapy, Carluccio's, Advanced Night Repair, Cath Kidston, *Grazia*, cupcakes and anything else that depends on women having a tiny bit of pocket money? There are mothers out there who will literally never get their legs waxed again which means more marriages in trouble, and then more benefit to pay, which is hardly a saving. Hopeless.

Honestly I said to Mummy, what planet are the boys on? Have they ever actually met a trophy wife? Because for thousands of them child benefit is literally the only money they can call their own, at least until they get divorced. Sometimes you do wonder if Oik knows about anything except wallpaper.

But what is maddening if you happen to have spent weeks sourcing a camel coat that is bang on trend but cheap enough not to upset all the poor people who are sadly just about to lose their jobs, so heartbreaking, is the fact they now all hate you anyway thanks to Oik, so you might as well have gone to Joseph if not Prada.

So it has not been such a fun conference which is kind of sad because everyone says Birmingham is so real. But Dave says no worries, babes, we'll be back.

SAM CAM SHOWS IT'S NOT ALL CUTS
AND AUSTERITY AT TORY CONFERENCE
AS SHE DAZZLES IN £750 PAUL SMITH
DRESS

Daily Mail, 7 October 2010

The National Magazine Company celebrated 100 years in the UK on Sunday by unveiling a list of the country's 100 most influential women. *Harry Potter* author J. K. Rowling topped the list. Runner-up Victoria Beckham, the Queen, singer Cheryl Cole and the Prime Minister's wife Samantha Cameron were among others in the top ten.

New Statesman, 11 October 2010

This week saw the launch of Viscountess Astor's new three-storey, furniture-cum-lifestyle emporium on London's Fulham Road. Oka has been marketing upper-class taste to the middle-class masses since 1999. 'In the new store we aim to give people ideas and inspiration,' she says. 'I'm a huge fan of neutrals, brightened up with keynote colours.'

Daily Telegraph, 30 September 2010

13 October 2010

People keep congratulating me because a funny little
magazine called *Good Housekeeping* says I am the
sixth most influential woman in Britain. I'm like oh marv,
thank you, brilliant etc but to be honest, I said to
Mummy, I'm slightly whatever, because aren't most of
their articles about cheese? Plus how much do good
housekeepers actually spend on handbags? Though I
suppose you could do one out of dusters. Luckily they
love throws and horrible Oriental rubbish so Mummy
said it's brilliant for Oka branding-wise, which reminded
her I still haven't seen the new shop so I had to ring off.

But if you're banging on about fairness, which is
absolutely all anyone ever does these days when it isn't
the price of my frocks, so deadly, it does not seem fair
at all that I have been put after Victoria Beckham. Plus
I think I might mostly be there because of Dave, which
is not totally a compliment, because if it was for fashion
how come I didn't come before VB, and if not excuse me
but that is not very polite of the good housekeepers is
it? And if I am so influential how come Govey's new
literary society, which is called the New Augustans, has
to meet in our flat even when they know literally

everything in it is brand new, which so is unfair, I mean even with his shoes off you do not really want poor Picklesy leaving his sweaty imprints on the walnut, Danny had to follow him round with a mop. And if I was really influential Cable would not have dragged me into the bathroom to say in this stage whisper Dave says you could hear through the wall, 'did that conference costume really cost £749, you could have bought a degree in economics for that'. So Willetts very sweetly pointed out that anyone capable of basic long division would realise that a Paul Smith dress would in fact not even pay for a module at the University of the South Bank, at current prices.

But Honest Phil said Paul Smith should have been effing paying me to wear some crap he knocked up in Biafra for £2.50, Topshop would have done me a bogof for cash, where's the loyalty? I just kept nodding and saying *eheu* which is kind of Roman for OMG, because Govey wants the New Augustans to talk as much as possible in Latin like the old grammar schools.

Apparently it is not unusual for literary events to end in tears because people get so terribly passionate, but I was a bit worried because Govey left after we drew for the first book without even saying *valete*. But Dave sweetly went don't worry babes, of course Govey can be oversensitive but he should have said before we all put our suggestions in the hat that they had to be before 1800, and anyway everybody loves Jilly Cooper.

BABES - these are the minutes from the spending brainstorm - soz, it was quite late, can't remember exactly what got OK'd, have put in all the legible/repeatable ones!

OIK - public playgrounds absolutely totally bloody pointless when you consider no. of fat people: sell or charge for use of. Pilot scheme? Suggested fiver (tenner?) per session, volunteers to collect.

PICKLES - Wandsworth already pioneering. Plus was it just him or is it obvs most people can't be doing with organised sport, since they always give up in the end? Senseless waste of time and money: cut.

GOVEY - in hand.

VAIZEY - what is the point of orchestras, don't they make an awful racket?

ME: Nancy is learning the violin.

HAGUEY — anyone here ever actually drink their 'free' school milk?

WILLETTS — agreed, classic babyboomer indulgence: cut.

THERESA — show of hands on who ever wanted to be a special policeman? All hands up. Proved you could run the police force entirely on volunteers.

OIK — brilliant, could we do the same with the army.

FOXY — would rather cut housing benefit first.

OIK — in hand. Apropos wars: aircraft carriers — couldn't we just borrow when needed, like streetcar?

FOXY — in hand.

HAGUEY — anyone actually listen to World Service? Everyone was like, wotevs: cut.

VAIZEY — show of hands on who reads books except for work. so: libraries pointless cos everyone uses ebooks and does stuff online anyway, cut.

VAIZEY — obvs, kids hate reading. So how mad are free books?

GOVEY — in hand.

FELLOWES — show of hands on who last went into a post office? Cos he has not been in one since 1964 and Lady F says no one she knows has EVER set foot in one. QED: sell?

OIK — in hand.

LETWIN — turn unwanted bodies into cheap energy?

PICKLES — pilot scheme approved.

LETWIN — anyone travel by boat nowadays? sell off ports, eg Dover?

OIK — in hand.

TAMARA — anyone sensible charges for work experience. Auction some fab internships to highest bidders?

ANYA — has actually organised, thank you very much.

CAROLINE — forests, anyone? Dark and depressing. Sell? Carried nem con.

VAIZEY — what exactly is the point of art? At least get volunteers to run galleries, if they're so keen?

DAVE — yes but saatchi support still useful: review next year.

HILTO — has anyone actually been listening to a word about the Big society? This whole meeting is basically like reinventing the wheel.

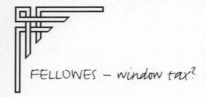

FELLOWES — window tax?

WILLETTS — handbag tax?

ANYA — over her dead body.

WILLETTS — coffin tax?

GOVEY — auctioning university places? Applause — carried.

PICKLES — do we need zebra crossings with their costly flashing lights, purely serving pedestrians?

OIK — genius, same with speed cameras, if people really want them, they can volunteer: Big Society.

FELLOWES — Hopes Olympics tickets not available too cheap, working classes much prefer skittles, has been researching.

SEB — rationing by price in hand.

OIK — Citizens Advice anyone? Nope? BBC to run?

HUNTY – anyone here go to the theatre, as in not West End shows? Could easily cut funding in half if no objections: carried.

VAIZEY – anyone EVER been to the Natural History Museum other than for a party or wedding reception?

FARTMEISTER – huge numbers of people dying, even with NHS: privatise?

LANSLEY – his idea, plus has already started.

WILLETTS – sell off residential homes with residents/children as sitting tenants? Still a bargain.

OIK – in hand.

PICKLES – Anyone else feeling peckish? Nightcaps o'clock?

Meeting adjourned at 2.45 am.

George Osborne has taken Britain's biggest economic gamble in a generation, betting that the country can withstand £81bn of public spending cuts at a time of global uncertainty and emerge stronger, fairer and richer.

Financial Times, 20 October 2010

The latest fashion name to team up with deluxe stationers Smythson is ... Holly Fulton. And who is behind all the Bond Street stationer's genius fashion collaborators? Step forward Samantha Cameron, Britain's new First Lady. She may have taken a step back from her duties as the brand's Creative Advisor, but she is not giving up her pet project for the label, and remains keen to support emerging British talent.

Grazia, 19 July 2010

The chancellor, George Osborne, today said the BBC will see its budget cut by 16% – 'similar to the savings made by government departments' – as he confirmed that the government has 'struck a deal' that will see the licence fee frozen for six years. Osborne told MPs the agreement would 'help every family' in the country. He also confirmed the BBC will take on responsibility for funding the World Service and BBC Monitoring, and part-funding S4C, as well as helping to meet the cost of rolling out broadband internet access to rural areas. He said this will save the government £340m from general taxation.

Guardian, 20 October 2010

20 October 2010

Well whatever anyone says I am not going to miss the comprehensive spending review because, in the end, it turned out to be so fun, going round the big table at Chequers with everyone shouting out ideas for the last billion of cuts, absolutely hilair, and anyone who hesitated or mentioned bankers had to do a forfeit, which is why poor Cleggsy had to stay and clean the swimming pool. But when the gong went for lunch Danny turned out to be a serious cutting talent and did around £245m in literally ten seconds. I mean who knew that pregnant women get free bananas? I know I didn't, and if the BBC is made responsible for that as well as free school meals and libraries and the high-speed rail link and bus travel for the over-60s and the World Service and flu inoculations and free museum entry and Legal Aid for divorcing couples, well I said it kind of serves them right for being so mean to Dave.

But Oik went hold on people, am I the only person here who watches *Strictly*, do you think our middle-class friends will want to swap Felicity Kendal for universal benefits? So I had this kind of lightbulby-ding moment and said so fine, we make the unpopular programmes pay, so *Newsnight* does the winter fuel allowance, *Panorama* covers school meals, and *Any Questions*, which is just so ghastly, does Sure Start, but for heaven's sake get a move on because here comes dear Perkins with lunch. And Dave went babes, you are a fiscal genius, and pinged his glass and said 'Go the Coalition!' It was so history in the making.

It is also quite historic at work because we have never actually done a crystal clasp on a diary until the new Holly Fulton one, which already has these divine drawings and a scarf lining and a pale yellow cover and two ribbons, and I worried it was the tiniest bit too fussy to be completely darling but Dave said trust your Prime Minister babes, it'll sell, not everyone's got your taste. And he was right because the entire world has gone mad for it. So the only mistake was charging £295 when it could have been double, because from what Oik's saying the squeezed middle won't be needing diaries next year anyway, especially not high-end sensibility ones, like ours.

As Daisy the kitchenmaid opens up the house, a telegram is delivered. It is 16 April 1912 and the Titanic has gone down, taking with it Lord Grantham's heir, James Crawley, and his son, Patrick. So who is the new heir? Not just to the earldom but to Downton Abbey, itself, which is entailed to the title. Violet, the Dowager Countess, assumes Robert, the present Earl, will break the entail and make an heiress of his eldest daughter, Mary, but Robert is not so sure.

ITV press centre, 26 September 2010

Highclere Castle, the 'High Elizabethan' style pile, is undergoing a much-needed £11 million refurbishment to restore it to its former glory thanks to the renewed interest in the 50-room mansion sparked by the ITV show *Downton Abbey*. Lord and Lady Carnarvon, the real owners of the home near Newbury, Berkshire, have taken the bold step after being inundated with requests to come to see the home, which is the centrepiece of the Sunday night drama penned by Oscar-winning writer Julian Fellowes.

Daily Telegraph, 17 October 2010

27 October 2010

It's ridiculous, I promised myself I would never get really political because how gruesome was Cherie Blair until she discovered eBay and anyway I am way better at bags, but some people's lives are so literally heartbreaking that you can't just turn your back. I mean, even with the economic situation I said to Mummy, what kind of decent society forces all these poor girls to leave their families and neighbourhoods and live hundreds of miles away in ghastly suburbs, and she said it is exactly like *Cathy Come Home* before you were born, sometimes it takes a massive wake-up call to show people what is actually going on under their noses, and I was like, respect Mummy, who knew?

Of course Iain Duncan Smith is an absolute saint and families have got to learn that no house can be guaranteed for life especially if they can afford bus tickets, but honestly, every time I see *Downton Abbey* I am in floods. To think of all the other girls who are driven out of their childhood homes because of a total accident of birth, especially the plain ones, which is so unfair on them but no one seems to care. So when it finished on Sunday, I was still crying although it was such a relief about the stolen snuff box.

I said to Dave God knows this is not about me because everyone knows I can't bear pigs or Scunthorpe, and Highclere is actually lol hideous, as for the bathrooms let's not go there, but can't we do something to help these people? So Dave stopped texting, which is always comforting, and said wait till I tell Nick about this babes, you are positively my favourite progressive, consider it done. And he thought Fishknife Fellowes could come up with a plan because after all he is the one who has got everyone so terribly worked up, but Mrs Fishknife was, like, over her dead body because apparently the only thing more vulgar than primogeniture is politics unless you actually are the Prime Minister, or just possibly, she thinks, a life peer. So it is quite convenient that Dave is going to make a whole lot of new ones, just as soon as he's modernised the welfare state.

'Angela Merkel loves Chequers,' confided one diplomat, who said it brought to mind one of the Chancellor's favourite television programmes: 'The countryside reminds her of *Midsomer Murders*.'

Financial Times, 1 November 2010

It emerged recently that the personal assistant of Mr Cameron's wife Samantha is also paid for by the taxpayer. Isabel Spearman works four days a week, looking after her diary, correspondence and clothes.

Daily Mail, 3 November 2010

David Cameron was at the centre of more controversy tonight over the appointment of another of his 'vanity' staff to a Whitehall post.

A filmmaker who produced his 'WebCameron' videos before the election has been given a public post.

The revelation came a day after it emerged that Mr Cameron had found a job for the man who was his personal photographer in opposition.

Daily Mail, 4 November 2010

3 November 2010

I know it's weird but until last weekend I had never properly met any Germans besides Karl Lagerfeld, and Dave said I should put him totally out of my mind, because Lagerfeld has practically gone French and the whole point of sucking up to the Merkels is to make the huns like us more than they like the frogs, if I have got that the right way round. Anyway thank God for Bells, whatever the papers say, because if she wasn't on the staff, being paid a total pittance, I would so like to know who would have let us into an amazing diplomatic secret – Germans adore sausages! Who knew? So Perkins ordered lots of the slimy tinned ones which are their fave kind, Bells says, it said so in an old *Dads' Army*, and we ran the Chequers menu past Heidi Klum, who is basically the world's most powerful German, Isabel says, and she was like don't forget the sauerkraut, plus mustard – not the seedy French kind, and we positively must not mention the war which was a bit duh, who do you think I am, Harriet Harman, since it happened way before I was born.

Worrying moment when I was getting dressed and

thought OMG poppies! – equals the war, equals *verboten*. But Bells, who never forgets accessories and receives absolutely no credit, so unfair, had already ordered one of those new Swarovski ones which could be remembering the war dead but could just as easily be a bespoke evening corsage. So, after Nicky filmed Andy snapping us all sharing a joke we went through for sausages and the Merkels looked amazed probably because no English person has ever made an effort with Germans like that, or not since the Mitfords who Angela hadn't met, such an incredible family, Mummy says, except for the very tragic fascism, not that they came close to the Mosleys or the Windsor-Mountbattens.

Dinner was quite sticky, actually, even with Isabel's list of German conversational topics, because Mr Merkel, who is called Dr Sauer, claims to be a Wagner fan but had never heard of the X-Factor or of Simon Cowell and there is only so much you can say about Birkenstocks. Plus they were both obsessed with *Midsomer Murders* which was not very considerate because, like Bells says, it is really such specialised, old-people porn, it is not that different from talking about the war – time to move on, people?

But not to worry because what matters is Nicky's pictures which Dave says are totally iconic, job done, and Isabel agrees.

DAVE – CAN YOU LOOK? ISABEL'S JOB DESCRIPTION – HAVE I LEFT ANYTHING OUT?

Dear Bells,

It is SOOO TOTALLY BRILLIANT that you can finally join us full-time, it turns out the special adviser budget will definitely cover you – and apparently you are something of a first, because it is the first time a fashion PR with no political experience has ever become a special adviser in Downing Street, how amazing is that? And it kind of explains some of my predecessors' outfits, no?

The downside, i'm afraid, is you would not be able to do any more work for Mummy or for Anya, because Hilto says it would not be a good look if you were doing PR for wardrobes and handbags and me all at the same time – so lucky me, bad luck Mummy and Anya! Of course they are both

<u>completely</u> furious, Mummy says you are the best PR <u>ever</u>, she really thought those lifesize leather rhinoceros lamps would never shift, but thanks to you and the Goveys they have a waiting list!

And, darl, just to recap on what I told you earlier, Dave leads the Conservatives, who are generally the kind of richer, better-educated ones, these days some even wear quite nice suits, the Labour ones mainly have adenoidal accents and awful hair! But there is tons more detail about this on Wikipedia and Govey is going to lend you his copy of <u>The Dangerous Book for Boys</u> which has a whole section on democracy, which is what we have in England.

As discussed, your main duties would be these:

Protecting the children and me from press intrusion. The media must understand I am a trained professional with a totally separate identity.

Organising my personal publicity, promotional appearances for the party, public family events, etc. Mostly stuff like cupcakes, children, tame pensioners, fashion, poss young offenders, Hilto says anything that's the opposite of 'nasty', ie, nice.

Keeping my diary (the damson with croc trim one, not the pink one).

Sourcing presents. Obvs the Anya bag for Carla Bruni was a brilliant idea, back then, but now people kind of know you were her PR maybe we move on (just ignore Anya on this)?

Wrapping presents, including large and difficult-shaped ones.

Going shopping. Need clothes for all formal occasions plus routine, über-natural photoshoots, stuff on beaches etc.

Helping prepare for state visits from people. Eg, we have the Germans coming to stay. God knows what they eat or talk about — try Wikipedia? And Govey is sweetly bringing in a copy of <u>Biggles Goes to War</u>.

If you ask the Foreign Office anything they will bore you literally to death, so don't, EVER

Then it is just basically the normal, basic PR ie, not talking to anyone except for News International. Remind me to give you Rebekah's number. Btw, you'll find you never have to talk to Andy, he has this amazing knack of just knowing what you're thinking.

blah blah love, me.

PS Hilto says sorry, not a good idea for you to say you are a 'sunglasses whore' any more, although it was utterly rolf hysterical when you said it in <u>Vogue</u>.

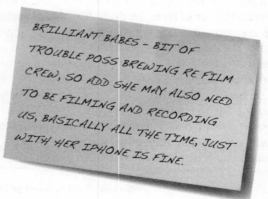

BRILLIANT BABES - BIT OF TROUBLE POSS BREWING RE FILM CREW, SO ADD SHE MAY ALSO NEED TO BE FILMING AND RECORDING US, BASICALLY ALL THE TIME, JUST WITH HER IPHONE IS FINE.

With Jimmy Choo almost a byword for high heels, and Anya Hindmarch bags coveted the world over, it's safe to say that the two brands together represent the best of British design. So who better, then, than Tamara Mellon and Anya Hindmarch for the Prime Minister to appoint to promote the country's booming fashion industry overseas?

Daily Mail, 9 November 2010

Not many of the captains of industry enlisted by the Prime Minister to bang the drum for British business can lay claim to nude photoshoots, drug addiction and suing their own mothers. But welcome to the 'fashbassador', as described by the women's magazine *Grazia*.

In her five-inch heels the Jimmy Choo founder Tamara Mellon towered over the rollcall of usual suspects from banks and supermarket groups that made up the coalition government's new team of business ambassadors announced this week.

Guardian, 12 November 2010

It was sooo predictable but still the tiniest bit upsetting, tbh, that everyone would freak about the new global fashion envoys because as soon as everyone sees the effect on the trade figures I know they will feel so blessed to have Dave and the boys in China, working their socks off for luxury classics. But it is quite boring being in the middle with Tamara going nuts about their hideous suits and shoes and saying she feels so let down because they are literally the ugliest people she has ever met, she has met cats who would be better fashion ambassadors and do I realise that Michael Gove alone has probably set her brand back by around fifteen years which is how long it took to make Jimmy Choos look edgy and sexy instead of just insanely vulgar and expensive. Well that is quite unkind because no one could have worked harder on his image than Govey before his China trip, look at his hair, simple but chic, and even Cable agreed to get his eyebrows done.

So once she'd calmed down I said Tamara you have to remember they are totally new to leather goods and just doing their best and it is so unfair to rake up all their old publicity photographs – how were they to know they would end up working for Jimmy Choo? And I went frankly, I do not think a person who has customised Uggs by covering them in gold studs is in a position to criticise anyone, so she hung up. Then Anya arrived and Cleggsy went and got our coffee, hardly a murmur, for once, and she says it is really brilliant that politics is having a moment, even if the whole thing is a bit vacuous from a handbag point of view, and Tamara should be thrilled that Britain's most creative industry now has its hub at No. 10.

Then Dave texted to say Anya's leopard-print Carker is a Chinese must-have and how are we off for stock because Govey has just shifted another 3,000 and Isabel checked the basement, and we were like OMFG because the workfare thingy doesn't start for ages and there are literally three left! But Anya, who is a genius, said relax, what else are civil servants for?

THE NEW CABINET'S FIRST MEETING

Who: Thomas Galloway Dunlop du Roy de Blicquy Galbraith, 2nd Baron Strathclyde – or Tom to friends. First entered the House of Lords in 1986. Jovial and known for throwing lavish parties with pink champagne on ice in the bath.

In-tray: Ensure the upper chamber falls into line with the Government.

Independent, 13 May 2010

ROYAL WEDDING: PRINCE WILLIAM TO MARRY KATE MIDDLETON

Prince William is to marry long-term girlfriend Kate Middleton next year, Clarence House has announced.

BBC News, 16 November 2010

Miss Middleton's millionaire parents Michael and Carole, who is a former air hostess, run a mail-order business called Party Pieces which sells toys and party paraphernalia.

Daily Record, 16 November 2010

The government will attempt to measure the happiness of UK citizens, it is expected to announce later this month. The Office for National Statistics is to devise questions for a household survey, to be carried out up to four times a year. This follows calls by David Cameron, when leader of the opposition, to look at 'general wellbeing', arguing there was 'more to life than money'.

BBC News, 15 November 2010

17 November 2010

Well the big day started quite badly because Dave said I had to tell Isabel to tell Anya that he is not at all keen on a Hindmarch pop-up shop in No. 10, even if Oik hardly uses the flat, and so she said well, wave goodbye to any Christmas discounts, bitch, and Bells was like, fine by me, girlfriend, when there was all this banging and shouting downstairs and of course we thought it was just Tommy Strathclyde lighting farts, but then Dave came rushing up yelling about William and his shop assistant, totally OMG. And although it is awful for the poor Queen, because honestly have you seen the parents, it is so brilliant for us that all the boys were cheering and Dave was like, hallelujah, we are fucking saved my friends, and Cleggsy was weeping with joy and we opened some fizz and the Fartmeister sprayed everyone and Govey led us through *God Save the Queen* because, like Dave said, it really was a dream come true, the photographer business was over, ditto torture, the only thing that would have made his happiness complete was some of Milord Middleton's finest party poppers.

I was so happy that when Mummy ran round with a

complimentary throw and a catalogue, she thinks that Welsh hovel has got to be a blank cheque made out to Oka, I said doesn't it all prove that, whatever cynics say about wellbeing, there's more to life than money? I mean, I felt practically Bhutanese. Because when was the last royal wedding that didn't need bespoke stationery and jewellery boxes and photo-frames? So when I finally rounded up the global fashion envoys we were all on this total natural high, because the guests will need darling little daybags, Anya says, mainly neutrals, and lovely summery sandals, Tamara says, and Bells says there has to be a limited-edition tote in there somewhere, probably too late for Christmas but why not start a waiting list? Then I said oh really, I was thinking more of a luxury tribute, 'the Katie Bag', sapphire lining, retailing around the 900 mark – and Anya said snap! and Tamara went snap! and Bells said she could not be sure who had said it first so now we are all quite unhappy again.

At Bristol, she seems to have immersed herself in some of the wilder aspects of that city's life. Tricky and Sam were 'unlikely mates', he agrees. 'I was robbing houses, robbing stores, selling weed by the time I was 15. But I was a good pool player, so we often played together.'

The Times, 27 April 2009

David Cameron did a sharp U-turn by taking his 'vanity' snapper OFF the public payroll yesterday. Photographer Andy Parsons will no longer be a civil servant after his appointment provoked fury.

Sun, 17 November 2010

David and Samantha Cameron have cancelled their controversial trip to Thailand following mounting criticism that it sent the wrong signal at a time when the country is facing widespread job losses and spending cuts.

Daily Telegraph, 20 November 2011

JULIAN FELLOWES TAKES NATURAL STEP FROM *DOWNTON ABBEY* TO THE LORDS

Screenwriter given one of fifty-four new working peerages as David Cameron heals Conservative wounds.

Guardian, 19 November 2010

24 November 2010

Pickles will keep saying 'serviette' and with Haguey it's still 'pleased to meet you', and as for poor Govey, eating soup is literally climbing Everest for him, and Dave has been in utter despair because although those things shouldn't matter to him they just so do. Because of knowing people like Tricky I think I am kind of much more open-minded about being common, but I can totally see where he is coming from. So I said to Dave, let's just borrow someone from Marlborough for a term because, seriously, when I was there they could turn around a noov overnight, much quicker than Eton. Or maybe some random geek from St Andrews could teach them history of art, because of course it was the Fra Angelico Annunciation that finally stopped Kate Middleton saying toilet.

So it was just a question of which housemaster until there was all the idiotic fuss about the photographer and so thank God for *Downton* or I never would have thought of Fishknife. Who is way better than any old special adviser, Dave says, because we have got his manners completely free in exchange for a peerage, and it turns out he really can smell people who say pardon! Dave blindfolded him and he walked round the cabinet table and picked out Huhne as well as the Fartmeister, which is understandable, Fishknife says, because the Strathclyde barony is only from 1955.

Soon everyone was doing so brilliantly at not being common that Fishknife said his wife had kindly agreed to come to us for drinks, which was so trusting because she is hypersensitive about breeding and the Hagues were her great-great-uncle Lord Kitchener's serfs until, sadly, the Great War. So Haguey did a perfect prostration and she said how priceless, wait until I tell my dear friend Princess Michael of Kent, and it was all so fun until she asked where we were going for Christmas and I said Phuket. Well thank goodness Danny carries an Epipen, because when she had come round Fishknife said it could quite easily have killed her, he felt pretty nauseous himself. So now we are going to Chequers not Thailand, and I am wondering if making Fishknife a lord was such a brilliant idea after all.

WIKILEAKS: BARACK OBAMA REGARDED DAVID CAMERON AS 'LIGHTWEIGHT'

Daily Telegraph, 30 November 2010

For a Prime Minister and new father, finding time to relax can be tough. However, it emerged today that David Cameron has turned to a computer game called Angry Birds. Players have to catapult birds into a series of ever more complex buildings, crushing pigs in hard hats in the process.

Evening Standard, 22 September 2010

England's bid to host the World Cup in 2018 has ended in disappointment. Russia was chosen by twenty-two FIFA delegates to stage the biggest football tournament in the world. England lost the bid – winning just two votes and being eliminated in the first round despite intense lobbying from Prince William, David Cameron and David Beckham.

Channel 4 News, 2 December 2010

2 December 2010

I can't believe I laughed when people said being Prime Minister could sometimes be quite stressful because they are actually so right. Poor Dave really did not like being called lightweight and inexperienced and only thinking about himself – plus that was ages before he really did cancel our holiday in Thailand so we will have to have Christmas in the smelly old rat's nest the Blairs thought was so bloody marvellous. But underneath he is so sensitive, just this week he asked if I would like a foot massage and it turned out Cable really is a natural podiatrist.

And if Dave is lightweight I said well lucky me because what has Obama ever done besides boring on, politics is not everything, look at kitchens and the whole Issa debate. I mean this week Anya and Tamara and me have been like the Moral Maze discussing if there is ever any justification for Uggs, even when it's minus zero and they are unrecognisably embellished.

Although poor Dave was going ancient history babes, end of, I could tell he was too upset to focus which was such a pity because it was the night Gillian McKeith got voted off *I'm a Celebrity* . . . and normally we would have been going yay, loving the extreme humiliation loser. Instead he was just going pinker and pinker, and literally glued to his iPad, and I was slightly freaking because Liam says it is vital that he doesn't explode and playing Angry Birds just seems to make him worse and we must find a game that calms him down. Well I texted Oik who said Club Penguin normally does the trick for him but Dave was like so insulted because apparently he's already in Elite Penguin Force and Oik hasn't even furnished his igloo yet? So thank goodness he was off to Zurich because Prince William was desperate for help with this unbelievably taxing app called GodFinger and Beckham has been trying to Christmas-theme Doodle Jump for months, so Dave didn't get to play Angry Birds the whole time he was saving football from the BBC and they certainly did not think he was lightweight at all. Which left me on Cleggsywatch which is so unfair, since it is not my fault he is mad.

Protesters attacked a police van today as crowds swelled during angry demonstrations against rising university tuition fees. A group of young men leapt on to the roof, smashed the windscreen, daubed it with a slogan and hurled sticks at the vehicle which was parked in the middle of Whitehall, central London. In other areas of Whitehall there was a party atmosphere, with students jumping up and down to dance music as helicopters hovered overhead.

Daily Mirror, 24 November 2010

Students staged a sit down protest on Oxford Street today to draw attention to the 'savage cuts' that face higher education. Students held a 'public lecture' outside Topshop before linking themselves together with rope and sitting down outside the shop's entrance. The students held their protest outside Topshop, claiming that the shop's owner, Philip Green, is a tax avoider, yet still advises the government on state spending.

London Student Journalism Support Network,
29 November 2010

Almost a quarter century after their band split up, Morrissey can agree with Johnny Marr about one thing: David Cameron is not allowed to like the Smiths. Following Marr's recent comments 'forbidding' the Prime Minister to like their band, the former Smiths frontman has echoed the sentiment, citing Cameron's support for hunting.

Guardian, 6 December 2010

WHY I SUPPORT THE STUDENT PROTESTS

'A degree isn't for everyone, but we shouldn't be putting people off pursuing one just because they are from a low-income family.'

Lily Cole, *Guardian*, 22 November 2010

8 December 2010

At the fashion awards everyone was saying direct action really is the new black, sit-ins are so fun, and Tamara is having her Knightsbridge shop done out with actual students for Christmas, *jealous*. So how typical is it that just when protest is having a moment, Dave has to be Prime Minister? The second I got home I was like, really, I have to protest, just a tiny bit, because honestly look what nuclear weapons did for Katharine Hamnett, some of us do have a business to run. Dave just went sorry babes, the rules say you can't protest and be Prime Minister, as if, men are literally so literal. I can't even do the Topshop one because we are still pretending to be best friends with Honest Phil. Well of course Anya is über smug because she's created these divine totes with genuine student slogans, so you can protest and shop at the same time, but with a luxe twist. And Lily Cole is channelling Gandhi and Jemima is doing WikiLeaks and apparently Anna Wintour was kettled last week in Selfridges' Shoe Galleries. They say Vivienne Westwood might even take her pants off again. But the closest I get to a protest is listening to Honest Phil when he rings to say he knew he shouldn't of sodding got into bed with us, what do we call this fucking anarchy in the UK, the wife's going mental and Dave had better effing call him back or somebody's legs are going to get broken.

So we are sending Cleggsy round because Dave is still busy dealing with those Smiths now the Morris one is saying Marr was right to ban Dave from liking them because Dave likes hunting stags. Well Fishknife Fellowes very sweetly said what do you expect from people called Smith, but it was still upsetting because until Dave gave them a mention no one had ever heard of them, and now Haguey and Govey and Hunty all sing 'I'm feeling very sick and ill today', each time Cleggsy walks in, so hilarious. But Dave has just signed the Smiths' control orders and he is going to get Cleggsy to bring back hunting, pronto, so sometimes it is not so bad being Prime Minister.

Chancellor George Osborne has been criticised for taking his family on a luxury skiing holiday – on the eve of a VAT hike that will leave families across Britain struggling. The millionaire MP – who ironically announced 'we're all in this together' at the 2009 Tory party conference as he called for huge cuts in public spending – jetted off to Prince Charles's favourite ski resort, Klosters, for the New Year.

Daily Mail, 3 January 2010

Helena Bonham Carter and Tim Burton have swiftly become among the most coveted of David Cameron's celebrity chums. Mandrake hears that the colourful pair spent New Year's Eve with the Prime Minister and his wife and assorted pals, such as Michael Gove, at Chequers. Interestingly, Nick Clegg – who has known Bonham Carter since they were at Westminster School together and introduced her and Burton to Cameron – was not in attendance.

Daily Telegraph, 5 January 2011

Since it emerged that David Cameron dined with News International executives James Murdoch and Rebekah Brooks over Christmas, Downing Street has danced around the details. There has been no official confirmation that Cameron and his wife were guests with Murdoch, the Europe and Asia chairman of News Corp, at the dinner hosted by Brooks, chief executive of News International, and her husband, Charlie, a racehorse trainer, at their Oxfordshire home. It is said to have taken place just days after Cameron stripped Vince Cable of his powers over media takeovers and passed them to Jeremy Hunt, the culture secretary.

Guardian, 28 January 2011

5 January 2011

Well, I am actually quite tired but Dave says I must do the diary because it was our historic first Christmas and I suppose it is historically interesting to record that the Prime Minister's wife is expected to buy roughly one million presents for which I have had precisely one thank you, from dear Govey, saying it was his favouritest gift ever. Mummy says the other staff probably had photos of Dave already but God, I know what I would prefer compared with Gordon on Courage or those bottles of Stimulique massage oil that Carole Caplin used to brew up in the Blairs' Therapy Hut. No wonder there are stains everywhere.

But I have totally forgiven Dave because he sweetly arranged a New Year party to make up for not going to Thailand, which was actually so clever of him, because even if Phuket is miles cheaper than Klosters, I mean I wish, it would have looked way more luxe than Oik doing his Eurotrash number in that hideous snood, Hilto was literally suicidal. And of course Mummy says look at the wallpaper, what do you expect? But Dave's pre-Christmas text did actually go, chillax people, but keep thinking squeezed middle, and how difficult could that be, even for Oik? Hilto says just not smirking would have been a start.

And Govey got so into deprivation that he literally begged us for an invitation so he and Sarah could 'save on wintertide fuel' plus, even though they are both allergic to Ferrero Rocher, they brought some as a present, which is apparently an utterly non-hilarious thing to do among the less fortunate, who knew? Helena arrived in incredibly sensitive clothes, you'd totally have to have known it was bespoke Westwood, but she said she had never seen method poverty acting like Govey's and that was before he asked Tim if he could have his cracker present then left Perkins his copy of *Nudge* instead of a tip, literally a nudge since she can't read, though at least that means she won't miss the mobile library. So New Year was brilliant, plus we got papped with Helena and Tim and of course Cleggsy rang in floods, because it is actually true we stole them, but Dave just said tough, what's not to like about people knowing we have stellar film creatives for BFs, bring it ON babes. And Govey, who was brushing mud off Dave's jeans at the time, went my sentiments exactly sir, I understand Mr Cleggsy is also acquainted with the thespian Johnny Depp.

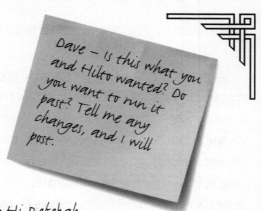

~~Darling Dear~~ Hi Rebekah,

Well, I just don't know how to thank you ~~enough~~ for ~~that amazing~~ dinner, ~~it will certainly go down in the Cameron household as one of the all time legendary~~ we loved meeting ~~the Murdoch clan, James is a complete hoot and neither of us will ever forget Jeremy's impression of Cleggsy's courting techniques,~~ your friends, it really was one of the highlights of our Christmas.

And thank you so much for the incredibly generous gift, we were overcome, goodness knows how you knew how we both feel about the Dordogne, but rules are rules and I'm afraid we absolutely can't accept, however lovely, the château deeds are enclosed.

I am not sure how to put this, it hardly matters really, but several close friends and neighbours also asked us over on Christmas Eve, and you know how touchy people can be, we would hate to hurt anyone's feelings, and Andy says you will totally understand, so would you mind <u>terribly</u> not mentioning to anyone that we were lucky enough to be with you for dinner? If you see Hunty, do mention it to him too — I know he is the soul of discretion but we do have various mutual friends, some of them of a fairly gossipy nature, btw do not on any account ever talk openly to Foxy!

Finally, is there any chance you could come over at New Year? Absolutely informal and cosy, and no one remotely glamorous, I'm afraid — just the Goveys, of course, and us, and the Fishknives and the crowd from No. 10, and Helena Bonham Carter said she would drop in, Andy has discovered, goodness know how, that she's feeling terribly let down by Cleggsy, sad because they used to be such good friends. And I know you would adore Timmy Burton, so terrifyingly clever and creative but such incredibly good value — Dave says he could teach Oik a think or two about the extreme right! And Dave is going to ask the Firths, obvs, the Clegg reaction is always priceless.

Do by all means bring James if he is in the neighbourhood, plus family of course, and feel free, please, to mention our little party to Rupert if you happen to be talking, we always love to see him.

Didn't the <u>sun</u> do a wonderful job at Christmas. Dave said particularly to tell you — we LOVED! And <u>The Times</u>!

With our best wishes for a very happy — and expansive! — 2011

samantha

Samantha Cameron has been included in *Vogue* magazine's list of the world's best dressed women. The Prime Minister's wife was hailed as a 'great ambassador for British fashion', with Vogue.com singling out the Erdem dress she wore during the election campaign and the floor-length Osman gown she chose for the recent British Fashion Awards. Her chic maternity wear also won plaudits. *Vogue* said: 'She's really clever at knowing what shapes suit her and she made maternity dressing look effortless.' Mrs Cameron's sister, Emily Sheffield, is deputy editor of the magazine.

Daily Telegraph, 15 December 2010

Our colourful Smythson diaries are helping us look organised here at Vogue Towers – even if we're not yet feeling very organised. We're already scribbling in the dates of the shows ... We particularly like the tangy tangerine flavour. Citrus tones are one of the biggest trends for spring/summer, as seen in our new *Vogue* Catwalk Report – out now!

Vogue.com, 6 January 2011

The BMA has accused the Government of 'charging forward' with its plans for the NHS and ignoring the major concerns of clinicians. Pulse reported earlier that the Government had dismissed BMA fears over privatisation of the NHS as 'wholly unfounded' as it pushes ahead with the vast majority of its proposals for GP commissioning. Commenting on 'Liberating the NHS: Legislative Framework and Next Steps', BMA chair Dr Hamish Meldrum said: 'There is little evidence in this response that the Government is genuinely prepared to engage with constructive criticism of its plans for the NHS . . . Most of the major concerns that doctors and many others have raised about the White Paper seem, for the most part, to have been disregarded.'

Pulse, 16 December 2010

The good news is, nobody complained about *Vogue* saying Smythson is its diary of choice for 2011, which was so dear of Emily and normally I'd be yay – win! – except Dave went appearances babes, enough with the Sheffield nepotism, got to be whiter than white. So apparently even if mine is Emily's favourite stationery, which it completely actually is, *Vogue* should pretend it likes another brand which is quite unfair on me because it would be fine for Dave's brother to say the Conservatives are the go-to party for transformative change. But I just went whatever, because the diaries have sold so amazingly, especially the tangerine one because of the new brights, and of course Anya is literally dying inside, even if she has got to do the freebies at the Baftas, because citrus seems to have totally passed her by and now it is too late and she is drowning in nude.

So Tamara arrived, very on-trend fluoro, and we had our first fashion ambassadors' meeting of 2011 and I was going how much are we loving all the tangerine ladies, thank God, totally non-swank, for careful forward planning and meticulous attention to detail, when Anya just got up and went thank you so much, so glad Lansley could spare you careful forward planners from the department of health, some of us have got Bafta gift bags to design, laters. Which was fine because I have a million things to do, like Fashion Week plus refreshing the notebooks for Autumn/Winter 11, because Dave said 'OMG' has got to be looking tired now even Pickles is saying it, and I was about to go excuse me and your big society is what exactly, when I realised how fab Big Society would look in gold, on Nile blue, he is so brilliant at fun titles.

So Dave said how about we swap, since I'm literally buzzing with concepts and he's got almost nothing for AW11 except for working the cuts vibe, which is so 2010, and Lansley's new doctors' health thingies which are basically like capes, so useless and hideous and nobody will want one. So I'm thinking a few stand-out brights, policy-wise, but mostly neutrals, subtle layering and a few classic, über English pieces for his older clients, a bit Anya, really, but with a more edgy, transformative feel.

The Prime Minister yesterday denied the North-East was getting a raw deal from the spending cuts. Mr Cameron made the comments during a visit to the region on the first of twenty-three 'away days' around the country. He took part in a question-and-answer session with staff at Greggs' factory in Longbenton, north of Newcastle. Questions on a range of topics were fielded, including the axing of the Building Schools for the Future project.

Northern Echo, 15 January 2011

The Prime Minister has brought in a fitness expert known for his work with celebrities to help him get back into shape. Matt Roberts, whose clients include Naomi Campbell, The Saturdays, Trudi Styler and Amanda Holden, was spotted putting the Prime Minister through his paces.

Daily Mail, 4 September 2010

This morning, *Tatler* editor Geordie Greig arrived in Condé Nast's London offices to announce what most of Fleet Street already knew: that he was leaving the high society magazine after nearly a decade in the editor's chair to become editor of the London *Evening Standard* for its new majority owner, Russian oligarch and former KGB agent Alexander Lebedev.

Guardian, 2 February 2009

19 January 2011

God knows whose idea it was for Dave to meet real people but I counted and last week some real people in the Newcastle Greggs actually got three hours more 'PM Direct' time than I did, and I don't think anyone even noticed except for Mummy and me.

And Dave was so depressed because as well as taking their pulse he had to eat one of their pies and went so OTT going mmm that is just the most delicious ever, you must give me the recipe, that he had to eat a sausage and bean melt, then a yum-yum and when Matt Roberts heard he was like, WTF, you do know Newcastle male life expectancy is forty-four, max? So then I hardly saw Dave all Saturday because he was burning off trans fats and then all Sunday he was re-reading Blair's book to remind himself why the NHS has to be reformed because unfortunately everyone has forgotten, although it would be obvious to anyone in high-end accessories that it just looks completely tired, just ask Mary Portas, plus Mummy always says that successful retail is 50 per cent familiar, 50 per cent refreshment. Actually I might lend Anya the Blair because she is so stuck with her tragic bow motif, and Dave has already highlighted all the bits about effecting change, as well as the sex part because we always act it out at parties with Oik as the animal and the Fartmeister as Cherie, lol hilarious.

But now Dave is out being Direct again and I do slightly wonder if it was worth doing the kitchen if he is going to spend the next four years droning on about the importance of getting out of the Downing Street bunker. Actually the flat is way smaller than any decent bunker but six months ago all he wanted to do was move in, so you would think Hilto could find someone else to do real people, at least while Florence is so small. And Mummy said totally call Fishknife, what he doesn't know about real people isn't worth knowing, look at *Downton*. So when I told him he just had to visit lots of Greggs and take their pulses he was so keen and said oh marv they are quite the most amazing family, *Tatler* has not been the same since Geordie went to the *Standard* – I mean, who knew?

Journalists at the old *Sun*, it is said, used to refer to any 180-degree change of course as a 'reverse ferret'.

New Statesman, 23 April 2007

Culture Secretary Jeremy Hunt provoked opposition anger yesterday by allowing Rupert Murdoch the opportunity to stave off a competition inquiry into his attempt to seize full control of BSkyB.

Daily Mail, 26 January 2011

The leader of the House of Lords went to ground last night after claims of sex sessions with a single mother who asked him for help in her battle with the Child Support Agency.

Married Tory cabinet minister Lord Strathclyde – a 50-year-old father of three and close confidant of David Cameron – was said to have pursued his casual affair with blonde Birgit Cunningham for almost eight years. He seduced her above a chip shop, had sex with her in his marital home amid his children's toys, and within the last fortnight stuffed £40 in her handbag before sharing a bottle of wine and a packet of smoked salmon preparatory to a naked romp in her flat.

Daily Mail, 24 January 2011

27 January 2011

Idiotically I didn't believe Rebekah at Christmas when she said how about a spa day, so I just said how lovely as per routine gushing, I mean we had been talking about horses all night and I had got into the habit. If I had thought the spa would happen I would totally have pretended to have scabies because we don't have a single thing in common except maybe Dave knowing Charlie, I suppose, and James, and Andy, before he left, plus the Fink and dear Govey and Sarah and everyone on the *Times* and the *Sunday Times*, I mean the ridiculousness.

Then Hilto rang going loving the girltalk my friends, the Murdochs are mad for it, and I said I would literally rather stick pins in my eyes but Dave went sorry babes there is no alternative, and I guess there isn't. And he said she couldn't be wired, not naked under a towel, yeah right.

So then it was spa-time in the Chumpneys whirlpool and thank goodness for her tattoos because it was something to read while she was going on about Sky and had we got enough godmothers for Florence. Her back is a *Sun* front page saying 'will the last person to leave Britain please turn out the lights', and there is Reverse Ferret on her bottom, weird but she said don't ask, and a discreet Rupert exactly where I have my dolphin. And she said I was well fit, had I done any glamour, if she had my gorgeous bod maybe she would have just stopped with the tats at the ankle, Dave's one lucky guy, even luckier if you-know-what goes without a hitch, and btw how well do I know Hunty, any special friends?

She did this nose-tap thing and I was thinking OMG if that is not a large beetle there is definitely a receiver in her hair, when who should come bobbing up between our legs but the Fartmeister, covered in bubbles, saying forgive the unexpected ladies, may I introduce Strathclyde's angels, my secretaries, Greta, Lotta and Britt? So when they escaped so did I which was brilliant because Rebekah is so not Tommy's type *sighs with relief*, and now that's the Murdoch pampering done for a whole month.

David Cameron has told MPs he would 'listen to all the arguments' in a consultation over hotly contested proposals to change the ownership of 258,000 hectares of state-owned woodland.

Guardian, 2 February 2011

Prime Minister David Cameron's communications director Andy Coulson has left his Downing Street job. The former *News of the World* editor finished on Monday, having handed in his resignation eleven days ago. Downing Street said he had 'finished what he wanted to finish' and had said a 'proper goodbye'.

BBC News, 1 February 2011

Nick Clegg faces a bleak birthday today after the Lib Dems plunged to a new low in the polls of 7 PER CENT.

Sun, 7 January 2011

Beyond frantic with London Fashion Week any minute and Andy leaving and Cleggsy so fragile, and Dave still needs a replacement Andy to explain to the public about forests, people can be so thick. I said why don't you just get someone like Daddy to tell them why landowning is so fun, he simply adores it and his enthusiasm would be so infectious? Probably a lot of people who don't get the forest thing have never closed a footpath or shot a rambler or held a kind of charming fête champetre as a chic summer party. Even Lady Julian of Fellowes says that woodland makes a very acceptable wedding gift, so what is not to like? I mean, unless you educate people, it is like trying to sell a buttery-soft investment bag to someone who has only shopped at Primark without showing them the hand-riveted quilting that makes it so worthwhile. So Dave said that was genius but he still needs a hack to bury the NHS sell-off, plus Oik has got this concept for selling traffic lights which could use some decent PR until people get what a brilliant hobby it would make for people who don't want to run a school or a library or a nature reserve, because almost everyone lives near a traffic light.

Then Egypt happened and Dave had to send Govey to cheer up Cleggsy. So Govey read to Cleggsy from Tennyson's *In Memoriam*, apparently it was a godsend for him during the awful elephant lamp business, but Cleggsy would not lighten up and come to Andy's party, 'too tired', so pathetic. But that was fine because he definitely would have refused to jump out from under the table going Gotcha! and we so did not miss his long face. And Andy cried and we sang *Jerusalem* and Dave said what a literal beacon of optimism, and all credit to the Fartmeister for his accompaniment but it almost drowned these weird sounds coming from Cleggsy's office. We ran down and Picklesy broke down the door and inside there was just the printer spewing out pages and pages and all they said was 'All work and no play makes Nick a dull boy.' Creeped us out, actually.

The environment secretary, Caroline Spelman, seems to have done the impossible, uniting left and right, crusty and county, young and old, effectively the Countryside Alliance and Stop the War and the whole 'Big Society' against the government.

Guardian, 31 January 2011

Obviously, it's just dawning on the gullible leader of the FibDems that he's been taken for a ride by Conman Cameron. In his non-job as Deputy Prime Minister, he takes all the flak for selling unpopular policies. The Tories have sucked out what life there was in him. He's expendable.

Daily Mirror, 7 January 2011

In one of his most scathing attacks on 'big government', Mr Cameron said: 'Human kindness, generosity and imagination are steadily being squeezed out by the work of the state.'

Evening Standard, 10 November 2009

9 February 2011

Cleggsy is no happier and when Dave asked for
volunteers to mind him absolutely no one put their
hand up until Francis Maude said he would gladly do it
for time off in lieu, because last time he looked suicide
watch was not in the job description. So Dave asked
Picklesy but he could not miss Pilates. And the
Fartmeister said his speciality is actually fallen women
if anyone knew of any, and IDS was taking Betsy to
Waitrose, and Fishknife said he and Lady Fellowes of
Kitchener are working 24/7 on their balaclava helmet
for the boys, which is actually quite a complicated bit of
knitting. Theresa has a painful verruca, Govey, Willetts
and Letty had a trainspotting commitment and Blondie
is finishing a speech called Goodbye Merrie England!
plus he had to wash his hair. So Oik did evils at Caroline
until she said she could spare a few minutes, which
only meant Dave had to beg her to stick to trees since
you can't trust her with anything, not even Cleggsy.

So I totally saw why Dave came upstairs this amazing
shade of pink, somewhere between our fuchsia purse
and the hibiscus planner, going the lack of human
kindness makes me literally see red and I said tell me

about it babes, it's ages since Danny did the rabbits and Vince has not even started on the garden, no one has seen him for months. And Dave did not calm down until Hilto came over to play him at Pirates vs Ninjas vs Zombies vs Pandas HD Lite, which was such a kind and amazing way of putting something back into society, because actually Steve prefers Boggle, under his t-shirt he is tremendously cerebral.

So how dim am I, I thought I would ask Anya for help, Dave being such a fan, but she went I am my own harshest critic and my biggest fault is doing too much for others plus the deal was high-profile global business diplomacy Sam, leave it. Tamara went hysterical going OMG are you for real wait till I tell Anya she will DIE, and Mummy said oh dear I think that must be my taxi, and Daddy said he could spare half a pig if that helped. So you could not say human kindness is on-trend yet, but I have put it in my diary for the minute Fashion Week is over.

At the Conservatives' Black and White Party, millionaire Tory supporters paid around £3,000 each for their children to have the golden chance of spending a week or two with a number of top finance companies and banks.

Daily Mail, 13 February 2011

David Cameron says it is his 'mission' in politics to make the Big Society succeed – amid claims it is being wrecked by spending cuts. The Prime Minister told social entrepreneurs the initiative would get all his 'passion' over the five-year Parliament.

BBC News, 14 February 2011

16 February 2011

Dave is so livid about the black-and-white party internships, God knows who snitched but we can think of a few Lib Dems, MI5 is making a list, and he asked Rebekah if she would mind terribly not reporting it because of the BS relaunch and after all the BSkyB thing is far from over. And she was like fine but we should think ourselves lucky tbh, given no one had spotted the Honest Phil internship which was a bargain actually, six months as a non-dom would be a brilliant gap year, and the most expensive one, which was shadowing Tommy Strathclyde and came with an actual peerage and everything you could eat and drink and shag for a month. And Rebekah is right because when you think about the champagne jacuzzi, even if it was actually very sticky, and all those Neets fired out of cannons into the Thames – you could see Simon Cowell was so regretting not thinking of it first – it could have been much worse, press-wise, and no one has a clue that we raffled the Forest of Dean. The Candy brothers are totally thrilled and have absolutely solemnly promised to look after the wildlife.

So the big news was Dave's Big Society speech, truly

amaze, and he was so passionate in his white shirt and Tamara was going grrrrr, and even Anya who is quite cold went I'll have what he's having, and now literally no one can talk about anything else, which is lovely but also quite worrying. Because although I love the Big Society probably more than anyone else – except Dave obvs, and the Hiltonator, and Bob Diamond who is secretly so philanthropic, his wife has just got a pool for their panic room, plus I have done woodwork for it with some actual very sad teenagers so nobody can say it is just an act – it is so hard to explain, like trying to tell people why they need a crested pigskin passport cover, they just have to take it on trust. Even Mummy who is brilliantly clever says she has no idea what it means but if volunteers are going to save the libraries she will have a major problem because she has already put out feelers for the one in Headington, total Oka territory, plus they could keep a few books for atmosphere. So it is such bliss to be in Fashion Week because everyone is so über-positive and nice, even about chinstraps, and that is what the Big Society is all about, I think.

Dave — does this work for LFW thing? Anya and I have worked on for literally hours. And if I wear the tangerine frock and shoes is that ok??? Ran past Fishknife, he said orange is common except for christenings but am slightly, like, WTF does he know about LFW?

NOTES FOR LONDON FASHION WEEK SPEECH

~~Yay!~~ THANK YOU! ~~Man, I am just, like, oh my actual God~~ passionate about ~~handbags stationery~~ fashion, so it's ~~so weird unreal~~ a real honour to be here as ambassador for the British Fashion Council. That passion isn't just about how ~~a high-end luxury notebook~~ fashion makes people feel. ~~Ask not what fashion can do for you, ask what~~ it's about what it can do for our country. ~~Full stop.~~

~~Anya t~~ People ~~sometimes go~~ often say that fashion is ~~like, way the most~~ one of our most important creative industries. Actually, I ~~totally~~ think they're ~~total losers~~ wrong. It is ~~literally a matter of life and death~~ one of our most important industries. ~~End of. Job done.~~ Full stop. It makes really quite a lot more than ~~£100,000 billion, £1 billion,~~ £20 billion (whatever, Hilto to check) a year for ~~Dave~~ our country. It ~~really~~ sends out a really powerful ~~vibe~~ message about creativity – and employs ~~like practically everybody I know loads and loads millions~~ hundreds of thousands of people. ~~Full stop.~~

I look forward to playing a small part in making this a great week for ~~the whole world Anna Wintour~~ London ~~and so do Tamara and Anya.~~

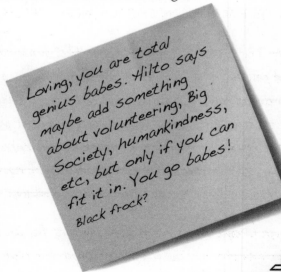

Loving, you are total genius babes. Hilto says maybe add something about volunteering, Big Society, humankindness, etc, but only if you can fit it in. You go babes! Black frock?

The Prime Minister's wife was British from head-to-toe as she opened the London Fashion Week season for autumn/winter 2011, at Somerset House this morning. Tonight, Mrs Cameron will host her first fashion reception at No. 10 Downing Street, for a host of industry movers and shakers, leading designers and the world's fashion press. Anna Wintour, the editor-in-chief of American *Vogue*, and Emmanuelle Alt, the new editor-in-chief of French *Vogue* are among the guests expected. All eyes will be on Mrs Cameron's choice of dress for the event.

Daily Telegraph, 18 February 2011

Hated by environmentalists and shunned by shoppers, the disposable plastic bag is piling up in a shame-filled corner of retail history. But a draft report by the Environment Agency has found that ordinary high density polythene bags used by shops are actually greener than supposedly low-impact choices.

Independent, 20 February 2011

This season Kane's use of unexpected materials saw plastic filled with liquid – vegetable oil and glycerine to be precise. The designer said this was inspired by the bubbling fizz of the liquid in a SodaStream and lava lamps.

Guardian, 21 February 2011

Shattered but in a good way because Dave is a genius, all I needed to do for the LFW launch was channel his BS speech and write in fashion everywhere he said Big Society e.g. 'I am passionate about fashion', job done, full stop, end of. And then it was so emotional because at last fashion was being recognised, they LOVED, and Anna Wintour said what a pity I did not mention what has been happening in the Middle East since she relaunched the midi, but full marks for trying and would I like to hold her used tissue? So I was fairly OMG – what, me? – because what an incredible honour when she could easily have asked Stella or Alexa, and Anna said I held the used tissue better than anyone, even Mario Testino, and he has this legendary collection which he is going to donate to MoMA apparently, if they promise to keep it permanently on show. And when Dave saw me with it he was like, what are you like babes, and Vivienne very sweetly explained that Anna's used tissues just kind of encapsulate everything that is so inspiring about fashion, from Chanel to Christopher Kane's amazing new liquid collection, which was literally to-die-for fabulousness, the glycerine-filled dresses sold out in seconds and Plum Sykes had to improvise with a colostomy bag.

So being a fashion ambassador totally rocks but it has a serious side because we are desperately worried about Kate Middleton and how she could easily destroy everything LFW has achieved if she keeps on refusing our help. I said the first target has to be a decent bag, and Tamara went excuse me, the boots should be the first to go, and Anya went loving the objectivity girls but trust me, Princess Primark needs a total make-over and btw Sam, how clever to wear that dear little mac to the Burberry show, had someone warned you there would be fake snow? But I have forgiven Anya because really what a downer to find out that your cotton totes are actually destroying the planet? And like I told her, who is going to buy a plastic one saying I'm not an Anya bag? Not even Kate Middleton.

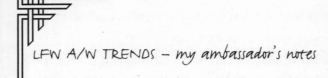

LFW A/W TRENDS — my ambassador's notes

KEY DECADES

Forties

Sixties

Seventies

A tiny bit of eighties — just between 86 and 87.

Victorian — not literally a decade, obvs, but still VERY important — see Marc Jacobs

THE NEW WILD ANIMALLY KIND OF ELEMENTALISH, FREEDOMY SORT OF VIBE e.g. panther thing at Burberry, foxes, lions and wolves and — respect! — actual real dogs at Mulberry, just amaze.

FUR FUR FUR! Everywhere! Except Stella McCartney, obvs. Tho' snakeskin is also V V HOT. Actually all reptiles literally to die for.

SWIMMING CAPS!!! SO ICONIC. Channelling Amy Johnson, in a good way. Or do I mean Keira Knightley in <u>Atonement</u>-wotevs.

EVERYBODY LOVING THE LONGER SKIRTS —

and the mid-length skirts

and the floor length skirts

also the very short skirts

yay — culottes having a moment! (Mulberry)

and also there are sometimes very short skirts but kind of worn over trousers. So, I think — THERE MAY BE A KIND OF FREEDOM WHERE A/W SKIRTS ARE CONCERNED

OMAG — THE CROCHET!!!!! (Christopher Kane = genius). This is just a TOTAL revelation.

KEY ADJECTIVES (talked to Anna about this, she says revolutionary)

Long.

short.

FABRICS

Prints are SO still back.

And so are dots (actually maybe I mean they are just still there).

And checks

And brights/colour block

And sequins

And crochet, obvs.

And tweed!!

PLEATS ARE ALSO STILL VERY VERY IMPORTANT APPARENTLY (but check w' Anna, cos privately everyone says they hate them?)

TEXTURE TEXTURE TEXTURE! = DIVINE

POSSIBLY LOVING THE NEW ANDROGYNOUS
SHOULDER? TEAMED WITH CHINSTRAPS AT
CHRISTOPHER KANE/PILOTTO, REFERENCING
YURI GAGARIN/JAPANESE KAMIKAZE
PILOTS — AMAZE.

DON'T BOTHER

parkas — so wrong, in so many ways.

COLOURS

stand out brights

whatever is more bright than stand-out brights

colour pops (which are kind of stand out brights,
but more popping)

and even more brights, as in fluoro orange,
tangerine, and that colour which is sort of

between orange and tangerine, Anya says navel
but I think actually is called clementine, or
possibly satsuma? (Ask Cleggsy, Dave says he did a
whole book on it.)

David Cameron was last night accused of using his Middle East tour to promote Arab democracy as a cover for arms sales. The Prime Minister was branded a 'disgrace' after it emerged that he has taken eight defence firms with him on a four-day visit to the region.

Daily Mail, 22 February 2011

Fashion house Dior has suspended its British creative director John Galliano over claims he racially abused a couple in a Paris restaurant.

BBC News, 25 February 2011

Opinion is divided on Craig Oliver's appointment as Downing Street communications chief. Tim Collins, MD at Bell Pottinger Public Affairs, said: 'The real question is whether Oliver is enough of a bruiser, and sufficiently dedicated to a Prime Minister he barely knows.'

PR Week, 10 February 2011

Well who knew about arms dealers because Dave says they were adorable, not necessarily NBFs but totally real and absolutely no side at all, as in one of them was genius at playing Smurf Village which is apparently unbelievably addictive and weirdly like the Big Society although Hilto says he has never heard of it, which is strange when you think he is never off his iPad. So Arabia was basically ker-ching, weapons wise, but a hideous schedule, literally for every tank they sold poor Dave says he lost a fortune in Smurf berries because the crops spoil within hours if you don't harvest them. And now he is back how typical is it that Libya is still on and the only person who is any good at Smurfs is Haguey? But he sweetly planned the airlifts around Papa Smurf's missions so Dave has already built three mushroom houses which is practically record-breaking for a beginner.

And Dave is desperate for me to play but I can't because it has just been wall-to-wall, 24/7 diplomacy since Kate Middleton scored two major fails in two days, a rancid old coat then this beyond tragic red suit, even Dave said it made him feel physically sick. And

Mummy wondered if she was delusional but Anya just went well duh, what do you expect with Camilla for a style guru – Wallis Simpson? But we are terrified because really what next, and Haguey said the ambassadors could have the Cobra room because he wouldn't be needing it so now I am chairing a Fashion Resilience Committee called Farc for short and MI5 have already traced the suit to a Sue Ryder place in Hungerford. So Anya is like, get over it girls, the College of Arms have already done the Latin for Trendy not Spendy, Tamara wants a temporary no-buy zone but we can't trust Jigsaw not to veto it, and Anna Wintour was just coming on the line to discuss multilateral measures when the new man, Craig Whatever, came bursting in in the funniest little outfit, think Baby Smurf in a suit, going soz to interrupt ladies but Galliano has just been toppled, I mean sometimes fashion is just crisis after crisis.

TOP SECRET — AGENDA FOR FASHION
RESILIENCE COMMITTEE (first meeting).

Chair — me.

Secretary — Bells

Tamara

Anya

Mummy

~~Emma~~ Lady Fellowes

APOLOGIES

Emily (having eyebrows threaded, available on
speakerphone)

Sarah Govey (wishes to be known as Sarah Vine at
Farc) — stuck at Chumpneys, could speak from inside
wax barrel if nec.

REbekah – going riding with Dave

ONE. Approve Draft Mission statement: To coordinate plans to ~~promote~~ protect ~~high-end~~ British fashion ~~after a major fashion fail~~ in any emergency or civil contingency, e.g. Kate Middleton, that might threaten ~~sales~~ services essential to the ~~fashion forward~~ community at large, to keep these plans under regular review, to report as necessary to ~~the appropriate ministerial committee~~ Dave. Or Hilto.

TWO. Qualifications for membership. Members should pref be professionally involved in, or be related by blood to someone involved in iconic high-end Britfash or beauty (incl. shoes & accessories, obvs), at least be fash aware at a kind of basic <u>Grazia</u> level, also, NB, not socialist.

THREE. Code of Conduct. Members must not wear/promote own designs or carry own-brand bags or request discounts at meetings.

FOUR. Meetings to be held in Cabinet Office Briefing Room A, or, if there is a war on, in the No. 10 kitchen unless wet (the new floor), in which case at Anya's (the Sloane Street shop), or Oka (Mummy has kindly offered to rope off the the 'colonial' room set, all breakages to be paid for). Plus we take it in turns to do the cupcakes, which must include gluten-free for Sarah, no dairy for Mummy and fat-free (Bells).

FIVE. The next meeting must be within two weeks of this one, any weekday between the hours of 10.30 and 12.30am, remember I always have yoga on Tuesdays, Tamara's colonic is Wednesday, Thursdays are Emma Kitchener's tapestry mornings and Mummy's acupuncture is Friday, I know Anya has her blow-dry on Mondays but it will just have to be then — can't they come to her, or I can lend her my Babyliss Big Hair at the meeting, tbh I think it might do a better job?

SIX. Proposed Agenda for the next meeting.

Kate Middleton: progress our intervention (military?).

Fighting Hat-use. Hilto/Behavioural Unit to advise on Nudge techniques.

Christmas bake sale (Pickles has asked to attend this session).

One of the few welcome side-effects of the economic downturn is that the spa industry has had to raise its game. Listless, half-trained halfwits spouting half-baked nonsense about auras just won't wash with a public increasingly short on time, money and patience: pampering just got Darwinian.

The result is a return to rigour: results-driven treatments administered by seasoned professionals in high-end surroundings. Luxury still matters, but we're not half as impressed as we used to be by a few fluffy towels and some free fruit. We want value for money, and an almost clinical focus, without the lotus blossom and ambient music. No one wants to shell out pounds, 90-plus, just to have someone rub a bit of oil on their back. They want a proper massage and practitioners are chosen for their expertise, not their looks (one of the best massages I ever had was from a tiny, wizened woman).

Sarah Vine, *The Times*, 26 February 2011

Could Cameron's friend Rebekah Brooks be the ultimate victim of phone hacking? For much of last year, the main focus of interest was Andy Coulson, then David Cameron's media chief. Mr Coulson's resignation last month took some heat off the PM, but redirected it towards his predecessor at the *News of the World*, Rebekah Brooks.

Independent, 27 February 2011

The SAS's humiliation in Libya triggered civil war in government yesterday as a blame game erupted between Downing Street, the Foreign Office and the military. Embattled Foreign Secretary William Hague was accused of 'serial bungling' after the Special Forces and an MI6 spy were captured and detained by a bunch of Libyan farmhands.

Daily Mail, 8 March 2011

God how dim am I because of course Rebekah was totally going to flake after the so-called chaos for BSkyB but I was actually at her foetid old fish spa with both feet in the tank before she texted to say she was gutted, sudden fungal infection, blah blah, luv u, so I would be all alone with the fish which is so disgusting as well as pointless. I mean I know Cable would have done it for nothing, and I am sure it was not even true because Sarah Govey is a famous world expert on spas and apparently fungus is the fishes' absolute favourite after verrucas and corns, they go mad for it. So I rang Craig Whatever to say WTF and he went we have total confidence in Ms Brooks except when we don't, so I think I will not bother to learn his entire name. Well, dear Sarah is always free and she was thrilled to take Rebekah's place because the Goveys are still desperately poor, sometimes she literally has to pamper herself and their goldfish bowl only takes one foot at a time. And apparently poor Govey is so stressed because of being up every night with his soldiers, he has worked out this genius way to invade Libya by digging tunnels from Chad, all done to scale with actual sand, but Haguey is such a spoilsport and won't even look.

So I went tell me about it because although it is such a relief about the new wedding dress and, utterly non-swank, a triumph for Farc, it was beyond nightmare persuading Haguey to get the SAS to find Camilla's dressmaker in Tetbury and take out her spare bedroom, plus they were lost on the Gloucester bypass for so long the Scouts had to go and find them and the dressmaker turned out to be the aunt of one of the SAS men so of course they had to have tea before they could blow up the dress and one of them got quite nastily bitten by her black lab which she had said was just being playful. But thank goodness we insisted because it was much worse than we thought, there was actually a bustle and a sweetheart neckline, kind of Franklin Mint does Queen Victoria, the whole country would have literally died of embarrassment.

Robert and Vincent Tchenguiz's flamboyant and aggressive business reputation was matched by their decadent lifestyle. With a £4 billion fortune to play with, they lived the playboy lifestyle, with beautiful women on their arms, and champagne flowing. Yesterday it all came crashing down as they were arrested by investigators probing the collapse of the Icelandic bank Kaupthing.

Daily Mail, 10 March 2011

Who should Middleton choose for the most important royal appointment of all? She should look no further than Samantha Cameron's stylist Isabel Spearman for help.

Daily Telegraph, 8 December 2010

'This started out over lunch with Dylan, actually. We had just started thinking about doing a men's line, so I thought that doing something with Dylan would be perfect. The buttery leather we make the bag out of is made at the most beautiful tannery in France called Tanneries Roux. It's pretty much the best, most expensive leather you can buy. It wears, and it's a very untreated, pure skin, so it changes colour with age. It's as good as it gets.'

Anya Hindmarch, *GQ*, 14 February 2011

16 March 2011

Seriously, enough with Kate Middleton, when the Palace called to say should she button her coat right up I was like excuse me I may be a global ambassadorial envoy but FYI some of us do actually work, Farc cannot deal with every single fascinator, though we did actually take out a whole consignment en route to John Lewis in Swindon which has got to be a win.

Plus we are already so busy, like Tamara says it is as if someone up there has got it in for upscale accessories. You wonder what we have done wrong because God knows who is going to buy all the citrus without the Tchenguiz girls and Japan is kind of a historic challenge, bag-wise, so we talked to Oik and he went soz, saving bonuses was simples but there has never before been a tsunami+meltdown in a key sector of the luxury market. And it so does not help that I have around ten seconds to create an Autumn/Winter manbag now Anya is pretending her Dylan Jones one is practically official Tory uniform, like anyone normal would want something inspired by Dilys which is what Dave called him when he was doing that ridic book, since he was so amazingly keen on doing our housework, the houses have never been so clean. Actually it is pure luck that Craig Whatever looks so lol hilarious with his 'Crumpler makes you sexy' messenger tote that nobody in the cabinet will touch a manbag on principle until Dave starts using my new one. Except for Govey, which is only because of Anya's 98% cabinet-members' discount and they are so poor Sarah says they will probably have to eat it soon.

So I'm thinking something very authentically English but with a weird-ish, edgy, post-nuclear vibe? For a name I'm loving Inigo, Orwell, maybe Cosmo? But when I brainstormed the boys Pickles just went is Bertram posh enough for you, Fellowes wanted Kitchener and Govey gave us half an hour on Disraeli and I was like are you mad this has to sell in Bahrain, I mean after Japan we need literally every sheikh we can get. Of course democracy is fabulous but it would just be so brilliant if they could wait until Autumn/Winter 11.

Cherie Blair has again lifted the lid on her sex life with husband Tony, revealing 'he still excites me in all possible ways.' The mum of four, 56, giggled when asked how the couple spend their time when the ex-Prime Minister returns from his trips as envoy to the Middle East.

Sun, 18 March 2011

David Cameron is entering unknown and dangerous political territory. He has already taken one huge political gamble in pressing so publicly for a UN resolution on Libya. But that is as nothing to the political risk he now faces with the involvement of British forces in Libya.

BBC News, 18 March 2011

23 March 2011

Well it has been quite historic because Cherie is still talking up her sex life, rofl hilarious although Mummy said she felt sick. And Dave said could I put in about being at war, or war-ish, for the first time in ages but he has to do everything because the Americans are so lame? Obama did not man up until Dave set an example and the maddening part was he had to man up with Sarko who is such a ghastly little squit and only doing it to impress Carla, pathetic. But there are pluses because next to Sarko Dave looks so buff that tbh you feel sorry for Carla having such a weird little husband even if he is a president. I mean when the ambassadors are discussing international affairs Tamara always goes God how gross is that for a woman who's had Jagger and Clapton, it must be the animal magnetism of power, and I am like, trust me, the premier thing wears off after around three seconds unless you get off on gilt and cornices, do not make me laugh. And having a war on is so tedious? Because someone is always singing *The British Grenadiers*, Fishknife won't stop shouting huzza!, Govey keeps lecturing Haguey on Clausewitz when he should be doing schools and Craig Whatever is permanently on at Dave to do a furrowed brow to go with his wartime smile, which I think is a bit matchy-matchy and anyway, forget it, the Botox takes two months to wear off and Foxy says Gaddafi will be history by then and those bad Yemeni dudes should be very afraid, because he, Foxy, is the man.

But I heard this thing on the radio about mission creep which sounds just like when you go on the Boden website and you think what rubbish I will just get one or two things for the children, and suddenly you have three tops, an embellished cardigan and some fashion backward dress you will never wear and it is too late to send it back? So Dave went no worries babes, totally non-swank but we literally rule, and I never thought I would write this but sometimes Angry Birds is quite a calming influence.

Samantha Cameron has finally captured the Downing Street rat – in a drawing to be auctioned for charity. The Prime Minister's wife, 39, did an art foundation course at Camberwell College of Arts before studying Fine Art for her degree at University of the West of England. And her skills are on show in the picture of her family's new cat, Larry, looking on as the rodent scurries in front of the country's most famous front door.

Daily Mail, 26 March 2011

'**I voted for the Conservatives. I live in a democracy; it's up to me who I vote for. And what I was voting for was a swing in politics. We've got the best government at the moment that we've ever had.**'

Tracey Emin, *New Statesman*, 8 October 2010

Excited! Because it is such ages since I drew anything except statement bags and I had practically forgotten I could do it and now Tracey Emin – tada! turns out she loves us! – says my sketch of Larry and the rat is so pure and totally what she would be doing if it hadn't been for all the tragic stuff in Margate, which is so weird since literally everyone has a house there, but Dave said you're forgetting Ted Heath, babes, majorly dark years.

Well, since meeting Louise Bourgeois Tracey has gone Conservative, talk about yay, Hilto was delirious, so it is now OK for me to give her drawing lessons and in exchange we get the neon piece, so long as it is fewer than ten words, which is actually perfect because it mustn't overwhelm the Banksy and the Gobshite. And Dave wants 'I go to bed with an entrepreneur every night' because it is seriously edgy and sexy as well as so political, and Govey will help Tracey with the spelling.

So I am starting with the male body in the classes because, although everyone knows Tracey is brilliant at anything between her hips and knees, apparently that is basically because she missed the lesson where they did feet and not because she is obsessed, and also why her drawings are quite small, because then people are less likely to notice she is not amazing at hands either, because unfortunately she had a cold on the day they did hands.

And, of course, when they heard about Conart, Tamara and Anya were desperate to come, but Tracey went sorry, hardcore artists only, that is where the YBAs went wrong, think of the Chapmans. So Dave says we can pick anyone to pose for us except Haguey and Foxy because the military would not like it. And Tracey wanted Vaizey but he still has 300 libraries to shut down, Huhne is mostly moobs, Cleggsy has body issues, Hunty is way too intelligent to fall for it and I was panicking because, God, look at the others, when suddenly, ding, lightbulb – I remembered Tommy Strathclyde in the Jacuzzi. I mean, totally relaxed even if he is enormous, plus being the Fartmeister, we can absolutely rely on him to cheer Tracey up after all those years of tragedy.

Whether Tories see the happiness index as a good or bad thing depends largely on whether they approve of Steve Hilton's influence on the Prime Minister. Hilton, the chief strategist known for his 'blue-sky thinking', has long been a controversial figure.

Spectator, 18 December 2010

Samantha Cameron will be among the millions of Britons holding a street party to celebrate the royal wedding. The Prime Minister and his wife have applied for a licence to host a party in Downing Street on Friday, April 29.

Daily Mail, 27 March 2011

6 April 2011

So next life class we get an intern because when Tracey told Tommy to undress he got so overexcited, we were like down boy, and he produced this bottle of cava and a £20 note and said plenty more where that came from, hilarious except then he was so cross he would not light any farts because he preferred to save them for the House of Lords where they would be appreciated. Of course the minute Tracey told him her idea for privatising graveyards he promised to put her up for the Carlton but she is still struggling with feet, so until she has improved I will draw them in the spaces and while I am doing that Tracey will bring some edge to the policy unit, because Dave says Lansley is a dead man walking and Hilto had better be right about the happiness agenda or we are all megafucked.

But I think people really will forget about sad things like austerity and Letwin if they think about happiness because we tried it at Farc and it was seriously a life saver. For example while we were sharing happy thoughts we totally forgot to feel suicidal about the No. 10 street party, I mean I have told Dave we will be literally the only people in London except for

Northerners and the Queen. And Tamara said the thing about happiness, like when you sell must-have shoes and you look amazing and you are on a beach at sunset, maybe the Maldives, with someone über-hot, is that you genuinely do not have time to think about your problems. And Anya said happiness is for losers but dinner at the Wolseley always does it for her. And Sarah said she was in a spa with Govey sampling a his'n'hers hot lava colonic with complimentary cupcakes and the sensation was so intense that for a few seconds they both forgot about the tsunami, and Anya was like, just try paying for it girlfriend, then see how happy you feel. But Dave's experts have scientifically proved that happiness is not about money, obvs really, because like Mummy says, look at the Kitchener-Felloweses, a basic title costs nothing and they are still in total ecstasy.

Cabinet Office minister Oliver Letwin sparked outrage for reportedly saying: 'We don't want more people from Sheffield flying away on cheap holidays.'

Sky News, 5 April 2011

It's not exactly Air Force One. David Cameron has whisked wife Samantha off on a romantic break – on low-cost airline Ryanair. The trip to Spain, an early treat to celebrate Sam's fortieth birthday on 18 April, was a consolation prize for the Baronet's daughter, who was forced to cancel a luxury Christmas break in Thailand.

Daily Mirror, 8 April 2011

The *News of the World* has publicly apologised to victims of the newspaper's phone-hacking controversy, saying that the invasions of privacy 'should not have happened'.

Independent, 10 April 2011

13 April 2011

Ryanair is unbelievable. Totally who knew because everybody is foul about it, but once we'd left this hideous departure lounge, because Craig Whatever told Dave we had to wait until some random civilian took a picture, Mr O'Leary just could not do enough, and I had been worrying about hand baggage but O'Leary said up to a foot over the regulations was fine and forget the weight, he just hoped we'd packed enough, with the intense Spanish heat. And they have this brilliant system where you can sit anywhere and O'Leary carries your bags on whistling *When Irish Eyes are Smiling* then he personally brings hot towels and champagne and delicious sandwiches and there was just enough time for his signature de-stressing neck massage before we arrived, then he insisted on refunding the fare because *Archipelago* hadn't finished. So I said to Mummy maybe it was a good thing we had such a nightmare in Granada being harassed 24/7 because it's like Dave's husky, now we never have to go on another holiday from hell to show how much we totally love people from Sheffield. In fact I reminded Whatever that Sheffield is actually my name, which is more than you can say for most people from Sheffield, but no, we had to literally live it, thank you O. Letwin.

I told Anya it was all jealous-makingly blissful, obvs, because she is still swanking about this new boutique resort in Rwanda where you stay in bespoke luxury treehouses among the gorillas, and Tamara booked as soon I told her about trainee picadors doing divine Spanish acupuncture, lolz, but that can't make up for the horror. Dave is in total grovel mode going next time babes, but I am secretly praying for AV because otherwise when will this ever end? Mummy wanted to organise some counselling, because it so helped her after that awful time trying to buy tights in Dubrovnik, but there isn't a spare hour before the wedding. But I have been feeling a tiny bit better since Rebekah got back in touch, going I do so miss our girl talk Sammy, give me a date for Chumpneys, and I checked with Dave and he said it was fine to tell her to fuck right off and I'll see her when she's out of Holloway.

THE VIRGIN FOREST FULL BODY MAKE-OVER,
TASMANIA — also near white-sand beach but
literally so virgin you have to arrive by helicopter
and what is so amaze is they guarantee that the
person who does your treatment has never seen a
white person before? Own personal interpreter. sarah
tried this incredible Forest Leaf Experience where
you are wrapped in a cocoon made of
individually — chewed leaves, which are smeared all
over by the local tribespeople and it completely
reboots your immune system because their saliva
has these incredible antiseptic properties, apparently

scientists think it could actually lead to a cure for cancer? Then they wrap you in a net and leave you hanging from a tree in the rainforest until snails have eaten away all the leaves or died — sarah says Govey literally did not recognise her.

TRAPPIST LUXE SOLITUDE SPA — in one of those ex-society places, anyway they used to have proper Trappists and now the monastery, which is on this incredible misty peak, only accessible by helicopter, is a spa, and the old cells are these minimalist but still über-luxurious treatment rooms, sarah says complete heaven, and their fishpond is this massive whole-body piranha-tank and the old chapel is a statement dining experience with all different types of porridge made to this ancient secret recipe which is apparently full of natural endorphins which can penetrate through every single organ so that you spend the whole week on this total natural high. The Goveys had his 'n' hers silent exfoliation where hedgehogs crawl all over your body, then they rub caviar into the weals which is apparently how ancient Russians always lived to 100 because the eggs are filled with essential oils identical to ones in the umbilical cord, scientists think they might really have found the cure for Alzheimers, and Govey said he felt literally ten years younger – you remember him doing the splits at Christmas?

BESPOKE ORGANIC REJUVENATING PARADISE – The other clients are a bit noov, blonde, Gwynnie-types, Sarah says, but kind of what do you expect in Hollywood – and they guarantee that literally everything else is 100 per cent organic, like the staff will only eat organic food, the building is organic, the food obvs, even the windows are made of organic glass and so is the cutlery and the leg-wax. Sarah says you can literally see your toxins being shed, apparently it looks like a kind of cloud, she could hardly see Govey through his, the effect is so purifying that some people actually start to levitate and scientists think it could provide the clue to human flight? Signature treatment is their three-day über-holistic his 'n' hers massage using Japanese essential oils applied with vintage ivory netsuke to literally thousands of pressure points, their antiquity gives this psychic boost to your energy flow which promotes so much cell renewal that your digestion can end up four or five times more efficient. When they got home Govey ate a whole packet of Hobnobs with literally no bloating or weight gain.

FULL-BODY WELSH RITUAL 48-hour EXTREME-IRRIGATION COLONIC — Sarah says don't eat much before, cos as soon as you get there — it's in this network of bespoke caves somewhere outside Lampeter — they take you to this kind of dark space and hook you up to the evacuation process, all totally natural and based on how babies in the womb do not poo for nine months, entirely logical when you think about it, and you stay there for two days while all the waste literally floats out and they refresh the whole system with water that is pulsing from an underground spring straight into your body, which is apparently how traditional Welsh enemas were always done before the English invaded. It is not boring, Sarah says, because you see all the unblocked stuff floating out through this glass tube, like watching your whole life pass before you, she saw an old Wagon Wheel wrapper from a design that stopped in 1982, incredible.

AMAZING BABES, BUT HILTO SAYS SOZ NO SPAS UNTIL AFTER OIK'S TAX BREAKS, COULD BE QUITE A WAIT – SAYS HOW ABOUT GRANADA FOR THE B-DAY? HE TOOK MRS HILTO LAST YEAR, SPAIN'S BEST-KEPT SECRET, ROMANTIC ETC. SHE LOVED?

According to Ladbrokes, Samantha Cameron will show her true colours and is 4/1 to opt for a blue dress for Friday's ceremony at Westminster Abbey. The bookmakers said: 'The Prime Minister caught the bookmaker by surprise as punters latched onto his morning dress U-turn and with his outfit confirmed attention now switches to his wife's attire for the big day.' According to reports, the Prime Minister's wife, and London Fashion Week creative ambassador, has chosen British designer Erdem for the occasion.

Emily Sheffield, younger sister of Mrs Cameron, and deputy *Vogue* editor, provided further mystery to the selected outfit, including a hint in a piece on Kate Middleton. In the article, she said: 'Will anyone – Samantha Cameron? – break with tradition and avoid a hat?'

epolitix, 26 April 2011

'I just feel it, in my gut, that AV is wrong. Politics shouldn't be some mind-bending exercise.'

David Cameron, *New Statesman*, 18 April 2011

21 April 2011

So I am completely forty now but I am not sure anyone
noticed since all everybody ever talks about these days
is hats, in fact you wonder what people talked about
before hats because although that is why I specifically
got Emily to write that I would not wear one, the news is
all total Sam's hat insanity. I mean, since when do
people not read *Vogue*? Plus everybody knows it is my
absolute, signature thing that I never wear hats. Except
for that hideous trilby, but that was just an Anya trick to
make me look idiotic and Dave promised to get the
pictures suppressed.

And now even he says it's just a hat babes, goes with
the territory, which is quite ironic considering he only
has to work his dark suit because Hilto wants to ban
tails, because of all the Bullers vibes. So I went tell me
about Hilto's uniform for wives, what if he went mad
about, I don't know, fluoro, would I have to wear that
too, even though it is so horribly unflattering? I mean, if
it's so terribly important, go ahead and bring in a hat
law like the Sarkozy thing and literally arrest all the
bare-headed women at the wedding. Plus excuse me,
while I am being forced to wear a hat Cleggsy is talking

about the end of primogeniture? Maybe I am being dim but I said to Mummy slightly what is the point of being Prime Minister if you have to wear what other people say, instead of the other way around? And what really majorly pissed me off was this delegation of hatters guilt-tripping me on my actual birthday, going Cherie was such a boon to the industry, when is it just me or are most people under the impression she singlehandedly destroyed it? Perkins says her hats got so big she left enough rotting straw behind to mulch the entire Chequers herb garden. So then they got out these feathery tickler things and said perhaps you are more a moderne, fascinator kind of person like Kate Middleton, and it was just Oh. My. God. But Anya almost died laughing.

So everyone is taking sides, Cleggsy is a no-to-hats progressive, so is Stephen Fry, and the Downton-Kitcheners say hats are common. But John Reid and Tracey are yeses, Hilto has converted Benjamin Zephaniah, and even old Beckett is sticking her oar in going no one will be looking so pray tell me dear what exactly will you prove by not wearing some stylish headgear? And I was like, leave it, there are some things you just feel in your gut.

THE PRETTIEST CUPCAKES IN THE WORLD

TAMARA'S RECIPE FOR VERY SPECIAL JIMMY CHOO CUPCAKES –

For the sponge you will need:

Organic butter – four kilos

Free range organic lard – 600g

Organic groundnut oil – 400g

Four dozen organic eggs (large)

Two kilos each of:

Organic icing sugar

Organic sugar syrup

Organic artificial sweetener

Finest Italian organic flour – one kilo

Three pints organic skimmed milk

One bottle organic vegetarian cochineal

For the frosting you will need:

Four kilos organic lo-fat cream cheese
Half a kilo organic icing sugar
Organic colouring (according to choice)

For the decorations you will need:
400g organic swarovski crystals
Or — for Fabergé cupcakes, six organic Fabergé
eggs.

METHOD

- Get someone to heat the oven to a very hot
  temperature.
- Ask your nanny to combine all the ingredients
  in a large saucepan and boil for one hour,
  stirring.
- Add more butter if the consistency requires.
- Then she has to pour it into the cupcake holders.
- Bake for around 10 minutes.
- When they are cool, get her to mix all the
  frosting stuff together then pipe it in swirls on

top of the cakes to look exactly like the ones in the Hummingbird Bakery (you may have to throw away several batches before you get this right).

- Now for the really fun bit – sprinkle the frosted cupcakes with zillions of swarovski crystals!

(NB, if you are on a diet, simply eat the crystals and discard the cupcakes.)

Makes six very special 'Jimmy Choo' cupcakes (she usually sells at school bake sales around £1,250 a cake).

I know what the Prime Minister does in bed. He told me. When he and his wife, Samantha, were on their recent two-day Ryanair trip to Granada for her fortieth birthday, the Camerons spent hours lying in bed watching a DVD box set of BBC4's *The Killing*, the addictive twenty-part Danish political thriller.

'It's our idea of relaxation. I think it's just brilliant,' says David Cameron. 'We should be making more television like that in this country. Isn't Lund [the female detective] wonderful? Lund rather reminds me of Samantha. Lund and Samantha are very cool.'

Allison Pearson, *Daily Telegraph*, 22 April 2011

27 April 2011

Well Dave said totally not to put in about Sarah Lund and *The Killing* because future generations won't know Lund is this feminist detective in the über-cultish Danish series of that name unless I tell them that is what she is, so I have, but I think it is actually fairly historically annoying to be compared to a person with no bag or hairstyle by your actual husband, even if Dave thinks that if she had some decent accessories and fashion-forward clothes and some beautiful children plus an alpha-male husband, a nanny, a proper kitchen, a creative job and a personal trainer Lund could be hot like me. And it is definitely worth putting that I would never say in public to a person from the *Telegraph* that I have been calling Dave Troels, or sometimes Troelsy-babes, and saying tak which is Copenhagenish for thank you, because that kind of thing does not remotely impress early adopters and now Anya will not stop calling me Lund and asking who keeps nicking Farc's Post-its. But it is a shame for Anya she can't see the whole mood board moving towards a more sombre greige/pewterish/Nordic/knitty/Killingesque/dried-blood/Bergman-y/Let the Right One Inny kind of vibe as a reaction to all the brights which are actually getting so tired. And tbh it would be way easier being a Danish feminist detective than chairing Farc's street party sub-committee which is truly beyond nightmare, with Picklesy going greetings ladies may I sample one of those artisanal-looking whoopie pies, do tell Miss Goldberg they would benefit from a tad more lard, and Emma Gosford-Fellowes fainting every time he says *scown* instead of scone and Anya getting all sniffy about Tamara's Swarovski-sprinkle brownies, the few Picklesy did not eat. God knows why Dave made him teas minister because he knows nothing about baking, I mean how bizarro is it that the whole cupcake story totally passed men by? Govey has literally never seen a cake-pop and Professor Ferguson could not give me the date Hummingbird started the whole baked goods revolution, when even Tamara knows it was 2004, and as for Cleggsy, I asked which topping he preferred and I said to Mummy, are we seriously meant to take lessons in voting from a man who doesn't know the difference between frosting and fondant? Someone really ought to tell the No campaign.

Osama bin Laden, the criminal mastermind behind al-Qaeda and the world's most sought-after terrorist since the attacks of 11 September 2001, has been killed by a US operation, President Barack Obama has announced.

Guardian, 2 May 2011

David Cameron interrupted reading a letter from a former Labour MP to tell a member of the House: 'Calm down, dear'. The Prime Minister had to break off twice more in his reply at PMQs, and the Speaker also reprimanded MPs about the noise in the House of Commons.

BBC News, 27 April 2011

The It Bag is dead! Long live the It Bag! In fashion circles, there's always a new piece of designer luggage to tote, but this season you'd be hard-pressed to spot it. With the overkill and overexposure of so many labels, what with celebs parading their goods everywhere from red carpets to the final of *Britain's Got Talent*, the style cognoscenti have turned to the last word in understated and elite accessories: the utility bag. Such a bag is likely to be quiet, casual, anonymous and – of course – staggeringly expensive.

Independent, 3 May 2011

So Dave was going calm down dear because it was 4am and Anya was in hysterics saying Tamara had called but Tamara talks such rubbish so was it really true because if so we must have heard, so I had to stall till I could get Anna in New York, but by then I'd already heard from Sarah who was at this tribal spa in Rawalpindi trying a complimentary full-body exfoliation and the person who pelts you with hot stones from this amazing mud spring on the North-West frontier had heard a rumour, and what was weird after all the build-up was, I was like, whatever. Does it really matter if the It Bag is dead? Because rule one for iconic luxe, though try telling Tamara and Anya, is make stealth wealth your friend. And then Dave's mobile went mad and he was shouting about the sheer awesomeness and it was even more history in the making than the wedding, with the Cobra gang crowding into the flat and everyone singing *Hey Mr Taliban*, with Govey on the bongos, and Obama rang and Dave went Waassup Barry, we're lovin' it, you're simply the best, Obama was literally speechless.

But Farc did not get much done because after a minute's silence for the It Bag, we had to have another for Vivienne Westwood, because she may never work again after Eugenie's dress, and another minute each for all the hat victims, apparently Tara won't leave her flat, Beatrice is still heavily sedated, and four guests have been admitted to the Priory suffering from PTSD. Then Anya said her bags have been brought into disrepute, and Tamara went excuse me girlfriend, not as much as my shoes, and they want Philip Treacy prosecuted for inciting hatred of high-end accessories but Mummy just went his hats have always incited hatred in people of any taste, and I said I do not like to go I told you so but what more could I have done to urge extreme hat vigilance in the era of utilitarian chic than ACTUALLY NOT WEAR ONE? And I told them Dave said they should have gone to Specsavers, but some people have absolutely no sense of humour.

David Cameron and Nick Clegg have marked the coalition government's first anniversary with a show of unity and a pledge to see out a full five-year term in power.

At an event in east London, the Prime Minister and his deputy took turns to portray the coalition as two parties with distinct identities, prone to arguments behind the scenes, but intent on coming up with unified policy conclusions that would best serve the country.

Cameron and Clegg appeared together in Stratford as the coalition government sought to draw a line under the events of last week, when the Lib Dems fared very badly in local and devolved parliament elections and failed to win the alternative vote referendum.

Guardian, 12 May 2011

As the Tories' chief strategist, Mr Osborne is blamed by the Liberal Democrats for authorising the No campaign's wounding personal attacks on Nick Clegg in the AV referendum.

Independent, 28 May 2011

12 May 2011

Right from the get-go Dave said Perkins was a mind-reader because even before we ask her to do something, like tell Lansley that Dave is still in the bath, she does it anyway, and by the time we got to Chequers she'd organised a cake, a candle and blue balloons saying One Year Old! plus canapés, champagne and kale-water for Hilto, who is on the Gwynnie detox, with the blinds down so nobody would tell Cleggsy because it is so vital to respect his total loserdom, Hilto's orders are keep him sweet until he gives the go-ahead for dumpage. So naturally Cleggsy was texting non-stop and it was classic rofl rofl, because when Dave finally called him back on speakerphone he was literally sobbing about AV, Hilto fell off the sofa in hysterics, there was kale everywhere, Theresa had to stuff a curtain into Fellowes's mouth to stop the snorting, and Dave was going 'absolutely, very poor show, Oik really should know better, well we live and learn', and when Cleggsy started bleating about Lords reform the Fartmeister actually mooned at his voice, I thought Govey would explode. And Oik was doing his tethered goat impression, where he loops his tie round a doorknob and does horns with his fingers, and makes this noise which is a kind of cross between meeeeh and Clegg, so random.

And Cleggsy started getting suspicious so Dave had to go no, just Samantha and the children, no that must have been Florence you heard, the dreaded controlled crying, ah well time for Bedfordshire, laters, then Pickles yelled 'missing you already', Hilto was so cross.

Last thing, as per, we did our happiness scores, mine was 'excellent – you are eight times happier than a married Bhutanese cowherd', but Dave's was off the Layard scale, technically he should be in heaven. And on Sunday Hilto gave this lecture about not smirking, Oik has to stay in until he learns, or wear his snood. And Whatever said can't we look a tad happy, sir, given you are the winning dude, but Dave went Craig my friend, if there is one thing I was privileged to learn at school it is the priceless value of sportsmanship, the correct place to gloat about Cleggsy is behind his back.

Emin used to upset the right with her provocative art and unapologetic mouthiness. Now, with her conversion to the Conservatives, she is in danger of upsetting the left. Yesterday Emin was unafraid of pouring oil on the fire by declaring that the Tories simply offered the best hope for the Arts.

'There's no money, the country is bankrupt so the Arts is going to be bottom of the list on everyone's agenda except that the Tories have an amazing arts minister in Ed Vaizey who is particularly protective and defensive of the arts.'

Guardian, 16 May 2011

The defence secretary, Liam Fox, has challenged David Cameron's plan to enshrine the government's overseas aid spending targets in law, it has been revealed. In a letter to the Prime Minister, Fox argued that creating a statutory requirement to spend 0.7% of national income on Official Development Assistance from 2013 will open the government up to legal challenges.

Press Association, 17 May 2011

Retail queen Mary Portas has been called in by the Prime Minister to save our high streets. David Cameron wants TV's 'Queen of Shops' to rescue ailing town centres.

Daily Record, 18 May 2011

Just back from Trace's show, she has asked us to call her that, which is AMAZE, we were blown away when she promised us another of her tampon pieces as well as the neon, and both of us are like, what can we do for her, because her support has been so incredible, totally unwavering, and I wondered about dedicating my new utility bag but maybe she would prefer something more luxe and while I am thinking of what – an evening clutch? – I said to Dave it has to be a damehood, because how else do you reward loyalty like that? I mean how weird is it that the week Foxy goes off on another one with the lame 'leaked' letter routine, and the Lib Dems just get more and more pathetic, although the Fartmeister says he personally is a sucker for Huhne's girlf's Radclyffe Hall/Ms Whiplashy vibe, the one person who actually sticks up for Dave Conservativism is a proper subversive artist with an anarchic sexuality? Incredible. I said to Mummy we did people like her at college and it is exactly as if it was the Blitz and Gilbert and George suddenly became Churchill's NBFs. Although I suppose it is fairly subversive of Trace to say that Ed Vaizey is a great lover of the arts, because the great joke about Hazy, although he is the sweetest, kindest person ever, is that he is always complaining that *The Apprentice* is getting too highbrow. Dave specially picked him since anyone who ever read anything would have refused the libraries job, obvs, and now it is going so brilliantly, Vaizey says, there are only three publicly owned books left in the whole of Gloucestershire.

Of course, after he read about Trace, Daddy rang to say how appalling, etc, apparently his retriever bitch spells better than 'your artist friend', but Dave told him to imagine if the Vegetarian Society started recommending Sir Reggie's Finest Lincolnshire Chipolatas, it is the kind of rebranding you can't buy. And Hilto is delirious because the Flashman thing is already brilliant, and now we've got Trace and Mary Portas who is one of the most famous lesbians in the world, he says not to bother at all about Foxy, or the boring two-kitchen story, we are literally so hot nobody can touch us.

When Air Force One touches down in London today for the start of the Obama's two-day state visit, all eyes will be on the two women – each lauded on their own turf as a trend setter – to see who wins in the fashion stakes.

Daily Telegraph, 24 May 2011

Its killer heels are de rigueur for Hollywood actresses on the red carpet – and this weekend luxury shoe brand Jimmy Choo was sold for an A-list price tag of £500m. The business founded by the eponymous Hackney cobbler and former It girl Tamara Mellon is being gobbled up by Labelux, the luxury goods group backed by Germany's billionaire Reimann family, for nearly three times the sum paid by its private equity owners four years ago.

Mellon said the deal was 'wonderful news for the women who are, or who aspire to become, part of the Jimmy Choo lifestyle.'

Guardian, 22 May 2011

The message from Hilto was keep it simple, nothing try-hard cos this is basically a relaxed partnership of equals, which was sooo easy for him, I mean he just had to dream up a Barry 'n' Dave promo for Rebekah to put in *The Times*, but at Farc we debated for hours because should I do a full-on, design ambassadory thing, or would that look like a frock-off, given Michelle's new adviser thinks she's some sort of fashion player? So Anya said go for underdressed in a way which could be laidback but could equally be saying excuse-me-don't-think-I'm-wildly-impressed-by-any-of-this-slightly-meh-tourismo-ceremonial, which is kind of my signature look anyway. Then again, Bells got it so wrong for the wedding and Tamara went, let's be real here, we're talking state visit not a pyjama party, bring on the Britfash glam girlfriends, and Anya went, well listen to the expert in nude photoshoots, so Tamara said given it was the sheer, unbelievable hotness of her naked English bod that had just scored 500 million for a few truckloads of already obsolete trotters maybe Anya should try it some time, weight permitting?

So after Bells had separated them, Anya forgets her

own strength sometimes, Emily decided the mission-statement should be 'totally fash-forward but in a fresh, natural way', ie, a LFW frock totally unlike that slut-walk routine that Carla and Princess Eurotrasherina of Marbella, or whatever, have both got into, Tamara says they'll live to regret it if Pippa's arse gets any more traction. And the Pilotto felt perfect until Michelle arrived in this blaze of extreme colour blocking, Tamara said it was so sweet, I looked like the au pair, but Dave went don't worry babes, obvs the partnership of equals thing is pure crap and your dress kind of said it all but in this really understated way?

The politics went fine, apparently, Dave said they have so much in common, they both wear boxers and white shirts, plus, amazing, they have both had an adviser called Steve, and Barack (apparently he is not keen on Barry) said they even have a shared ancestor from way back, this African woman called Lucy, who knew?

Samantha Cameron gets an itsy-bit daring as she soaks up the sunshine on a family holiday. After partying with hen-night revellers at an Ibiza rave, the PM's missus went for the hippie-chic look in a colourful 'flower-power' bikini.

Daily Mirror, 30 May 2011

With its immaculate cabinets, gleaming accessories and shiny pans in neat lines, it looks every inch the modern show home. But this is no artificial stage. This is the first glimpse of the much-talked-about kitchen David and Samantha Cameron had fitted in their flat at No. 11 Downing Street. As Michelle Obama and Samantha Cameron chat on the mustard 'Fancy Nancy' sofa – cementing the 'special relationship' the Prime Minister talked of earlier that day – we are offered a tantalising peek inside the Camerons' recently updated private residence.

Daily Mail, 27 May 2011

1 June 2010

Anya was straight on the phone going God how can you bear to be photographed in a bikini, why don't I courier over a vibrant kaftan from my new beach collection, and I was like, how can you not understand that after last week in the council flat, a beach papping counts as a win? I mean, at least when you are on a pedalo Craig Whatever cannot come up going, how about you lovely ladies pretend to serve coleslaw, act like you're sharing a joke, big smiles, loving it, two hostesses with the mostest assisting the noble veterans of conflict. With Dave just going sorry babes, of course he is a total and complete arse but that is why we employ him, have to do what the man says. And nobody even knows that Craig had us scheduled to lead a group of young offenders in an inspirational yoga class on a clifftop outside Dover with Dave playing boyishly with a puppy and Barack more maturely flying a kite that symbolised the Soaring Hopes of our Essential Relationship, but unfortunately Michelle had forgotten her leotard so we had to pose in the kitchen instead. Whatever said to act like two lovely ladies having a lovely lovely goss about worktops, why not have a little practice while he edited the bookshelves, and Michelle said to me if I really believed in myself and worked hard maybe one day I would be able to afford some cupboards, our simple shelves reminded her of her shy young self.

Of course Mummy was ecstatic, Dave says he has literally not seen her so happy since the Govey thing shifted 14,000 elephant lamps, because within three hours of the *Mail* website saying we'd bought Oka bookshelves – I mean, as if, with no discount – she'd raised the deposit for a new industrial site in Maharashtra.

But what is actually brilliant, as well as Pete Tong being so totally legend, is while we are in Ibiza they can work on the third kitchen because once 60 million people have been invited to bitch about a kitchen you PERSONALLY DONATED to them, it does not feel the same, plus that sleek, walnut/graphite vibe is already looking the tiniest bit over, kitchen-wise.

The Government has published the UK's first National Ecosystem Assessment today, a ground breaking report which attempts to put a cash price on the environmental services provided by nature.

BBC News, 2 June 2011

The Conservative Party was in celebratory mood last night after hosting its summer ball. Government ministers, MPs and party grandees descended on the Natural History Museum in London for the annual feel-good thrash.

Daily Mail, 8 June 2011

'For what you're getting, they're incredibly well priced. It's a forever bag,' says L'Wren Scott, the designer girlfriend of Mick Jagger, of her new Lula handbag range. 'Well priced', in case you were wondering, means between $2,300 and $20,000.

Independent, 7 June 2011

9 June 2011

Dave loves, but maybe I went too brown in Ibiza cos Anya said 'the future's bright' the minute I walked into the summer ball, but the weird thing is, it is. Because people are finally seeing how much Dave has learned from my luxe retail experience and even Oik grasps that it is literally insane to have Anya and Tamara and me around and not apply our knowledge of pricing intangibles, like L'Wren Scott wanting $2,300 for her small Lula bag, which is not actually unreasonable even if it does look fairly boring and clunky, because you've got to factor in stuff like the noise it makes when you open it. I mean, I said to Cleggsy, very slowly because he was really struggling with the concept, on the face of it, a high-end tree might seem fairly worthless, given it doesn't do much and you could eventually grow another, just the same. But it still has a value when you think of the divine rustling sound, plus the lifetime offer of shade, the range of classic colours in a whole variety of different greens, all the leaves that had to be specially grown, the exquisitely crafted bark, and the fact that you're looking at half the infrastructure for a hammock, if you favour the artisanal look.

Of course when it finally clicked about eco-valuation Cleggsy started going outrageous, how can you put a price on beauty, next thing you'll be costing happiness – I'm like, do keep up – and now he looks so idiotic because the experts are saying the value of nature is totally awesome? Oik thinks if we only sold off robins it would pay for the whole NHS restructuring without an significant impact on worms. So Honest Phil obvs wants a piece and Tamara says whatever we're selling, she's in, this could be bigger than Jimmy Choo. But imho we wait, cos *Springwatch* is still talking up the robin price and there's so much stuff left to value, a small iconic songbird might be practically worthless compared with the moon, which admittedly does not serve any purpose I can think of, but everyone said the exact same thing about Prada and now that is worth $15 billion.

Prime Minister David Cameron has mounted a robust defence of government policy following criticisms by the Archbishop of Canterbury. Mr Cameron said Dr Rowan Williams was 'free to express political views' – but he 'profoundly disagrees' with them.

Dr Williams criticised the coalition's flagship welfare reforms and branded the Prime Minister's Big Society 'stale'. And he said 'radical' policies 'for which no one voted' were being pushed through with 'remarkable speed'. Mr Cameron was asked about the remarks in Dr Williams's article for the left-leaning *New Statesman* magazine, the latest edition of which the most senior cleric in the Church of England guest-edited.

BBC News, 9 June 2011

The Holy Bible Magenta Collection, £175.00. An authorized King James Version, bound in Smythson Magenta leather, a wonderful christening gift.

Smythson catalogue

OMG, bishops. They have these kindly faces and grey beards, but underneath, man, are they angry. And of course nobody ever warned us about bishops, unless you count Richard Dawkins, so it was such a shock when the top one, Rowan something, who was all smiley at the Middleton wedding, just suddenly went off on one, saying Dave is frightening the poor, which Philip Blondie says is not at all in the Bible, he has literally read the whole thing, and now the entire bishop posse is after us. And it is so ridic and hurtful when you think of everything Dave has done for marriage and faith schools and Africans, plus actually quite rude since my signature bible is actually the first pink bible in the world, we have sold thousands; you would think any proper bishop would LOVE.

Of course Dave wanted to get straight on to the queen, given she is their line manager, but Blondie says excommunication takes years, much better to have them pissing out of the tent, plus there's always the Lords review. So now it is just like wangling a church school place when you know the vicar is a foaming lefty but if you go every Sunday with the Goveys and sit at the front and do the snog of peace and listen to their awful sermons saying how sinful and disgusting rich people are, they simply can't find a reason to oppose you, especially if you help with refreshments and they know you would go to appeal anyway.

So, total and utter gruesomeness, we had to have the bishops for coffee and digestives, and the minute I said OMAG one of them went 'I would prefer you did not say that', and it was the same with 'holy shit', plus they want me to withdraw the 'OMG!' notebook, even though it is absolutely one of our top sellers. And Dave has to stop spreading fear, Rowan says, or we might want to reflect that an Anglican education is a very special gift that is ideally reserved for the marginal. And I would normally have been, WTF, GTFO, but just in time I went 'oh my days', which works brilliantly as a bishop-friendly expletive, but I can't see it on a fun notebook.

The Prime Minister made a meal of an official engagement yesterday – inviting the Queen around for lunch at Downing Street. Chubby Cam and wife Sam were celebrating Prince Philip's ninetieth birthday with Her Majesty. But at least the Queen could put the Tory boy Prime Minister in his place by carefully studying photos of his predecessors on the stairs. Their pictures go up when they leave office. How long before his picture is on the wall? So far Her Majesty has been served by twelve Prime Ministers, including Cameron, two fewer than George III and two more than Queen Victoria.

As the royal couple emerged from their Daimler Super Eight, there was some initial confusion over who should stand where for the official photographs. But Philip was then guided to the end of the line where he stood beside Mrs Cameron, then the Queen and finally Mr Cameron. They were then escorted up the stairs of Number 10.

Daily Mirror, 22 June 2011

It seems there is no looking back for Pippa Middleton and her celebrated derriere. Artist and satirical photographer Alison Jackson is planning a series of YouTube-style episodes dedicated to achieving a bottom as perfectly sculpted as Pippa's.

Daily Mail, 10 July 2011

23 June 2011

Everyone keeps going what's she like, and I'm like, she's the Queen, how can you not totally heart her? I mean she is so cosy, not remotely grand, and actually not at all common, whatever the Fishknives say. What can I say except it was one of those properly historic moments when seriously all you can think is God, why aren't I tweeting so this experience will stay with me forever? Of course Dave was texting Clarkson under the table, so at least there is a record of Philip asking, man to man, what Dave thought of Pippa's arse.

Apart from the doorstep picture it went like clockwork, because Hilto had really wanted Dave filmed in a royal sandwich for long enough to bury Kenneth Clarke plus five U-turns, women's pensions and the Greek bailout, say two minutes, minimum, but my Philip-catching sequence meant we still aced it, Hilto says royals blow huskies out of the water. So we went in and Dave went how humbling, but in a non-grovel way, and we looked at the PM photographs and Philip pulled a face in front of Brown and Blair, hilarious, then it was lunch and Dave explained the big society, and the Queen and Philip just listened in what Dave says is best recorded as utterly rapt fascination, she was speechless and Philip focused so hard he had to have a tiny doze before pudding. Then Dave explained about broken Britain and why divorcees are literally worse than mass murderers, which obvs intrigued the Queen because she said she might mention it to Charles and Camilla and Andrew and Anne, who would be so interested.

Then we went to the flat, Hilto had hidden the Emin and Banksys, and the Queen said how wise not to waste money on staff accommodation, though without any carpets they might want slankets before winter sets in. And she said she had one question, did we know Boris Johson, because she and Philip find him just simply priceless, they are always in fits, was there any chance of an introduction? Dave was brilliant and said I am sorry to tell you Ma'am, but he lives the secluded life of a hermit. Weird, though. How could anyone think of Boris, when Dave is around?

After some disastrous internal polling, the Conservatives are waking up to the fact their relationship with British women is starting to go sour. In a panic, they've executed more U-turns than a dog chasing its tail as they frantically try to recapture the group of voters without whom they'll lose the next election.

This tactic won't work, though, because it doesn't get to the heart of what's wrong. And until it does, we'll continue to go off Cameron faster than butter turns rancid in the sun.

Sandra Parsons, *Daily Mail*, 29 June 2011

One of the admirable things about Caitlin Moran's down-to-earth book about modern womanhood is that she makes being a 'strident feminist' sound not just an obvious choice but heaps of fun. Moran at full force is a blast of refreshing (if somewhat booze-and-fag-scented) air.

Here, she mounts a hilarious attack on appearance-obsessed, celebrity-fixated notions of contemporary femininity in a book that's part rant, part confessional.

Metro, 5 July 2011

East Northamptonshire and Corby MP Louise Bagshawe (Con) has married the manager of heavy metal band Metallica, Peter Mensch, during a secret ceremony in Manhattan, New York.

The MP, who is also an author, has announced that she will be changing her surname.

Rutland and Stamford Mercury, 17 June 2011

So while Hilto did the focus group Dave got everyone in the cabinet room to figure out why women have gone off him, and it is so baffling because literally no prime minister EVER has done more for accessories. And Cleggsy said it was all down to child benefit, didn't anyone remember his warning (no), and Govey said rubbish, they will have forgotten, science tells us the smaller female brain is incapable of sustained analysis, that's why we only have a fashion week, not a year. And Oik said the smaller female brain cannot handle abstract thoughts such as new retirement ages, and Lansley said women were good as gold before hormone replacement, but the new HRT postcode lottery should sort it. Fellowes wanted to bring back governesses, Letwin blamed Murdoch for letting Caitlin Moran spread discontent, and Willetts wants Nancy Dell'olio to take over Women2Win since she is a superb female and role model, and Hunty is going to get her number off Trevor Nunn. And Vaizey said Louise Bagshawe has been such a colossal disappointment, practically a practising hippy plus she's gone and changed her name, how about another blonde chicklit author – he has heard great things on the literary circuit about this hottie called Diana Athill? Nobody knows what Caroline and Theresa think, because of course the Fartmeister always shouts 'melons' or 'Giddy up there Phoebe!' when they try to speak, which kind of saves them from themselves, Dave says, which is so sweet.

So the envoys came over and Anya just went what a ridic fuss about nothing, Mulberry's Alexa bag is way older than the Coalition but women still love it because now there's the Alexa Hobo, mini-Alexa, oversized Alexa, etc, we just do a bigger version of Dave, or maybe a more compact one, and they'll love him again. And Tamara said she could not speak for all women, and Anya said no wonder with your sales, and I really thought Anya was going to be scarred for life because Tamara had just had this Swarovski crystal mani-pedi, when Whatever came in from the focus group and asked them to leave. But they were listening the keyhole, you could hear these total hysterics when he said it was desperately sad but women are punishing Dave for my designer dresses. I mean totally so much for the new feminism *sad face*.

Until now it has been easy to argue that Mr Cameron was properly grounded with a decent set of values. Unfortunately, it is impossible to make that assertion any longer. He has made not one, but a long succession of chronic personal misjudgments.

He should never have employed Andy Coulson, the *News of the World* editor, as his director of communications. He should never have cultivated Rupert Murdoch. And – the worst mistake of all – he should never have allowed himself to become a close friend of Rebekah Brooks, the chief executive of the media giant News International, whose departure from that company in shame and disgrace can only be a matter of time.

Peter Oborne, *Daily Telegraph*, 6 July 2011

Police arrested David Cameron's former spokesman on Friday over the scandal that has shut down Rupert Murdoch's *News of the World*, forcing the prime minister to defend his judgement while promising new controls on the press.

As Cameron fielded hostile questions over why he had hired the paper's former editor Andy Coulson in 2007, despite knowing that one of his journalists had been jailed for hacking into voicemails in search of scoops, Coulson was being arrested by police on suspicion of conspiring in the illegal practice.

Cameron said he took 'full responsibility' for his decision to appoint Coulson, who quit Downing Street in January when police relaunched inquiries. But the premier rebuffed criticism and strove to spread the blame for an affair that has generated public outrage against the press, politicians and police.

Reuters, July 8 2011

July 7 2011

Well the first I knew about anything was Tamara going massive apols, her vajazzle had worn off like weirdly quickly and she had this nude photo shoot coming up so she would not be at this week's Farc. And I was like, whatever, since she hardly ever turns up these days, but then Anya emailed, going absolutely no offence, but her bunion person was insisting on total bed rest. Then Emma Gosford-Fellowes texted, which is kind of unheard of, saying she had just smelled a common smell, her doctor was on his way, then Mary Portas remembered a tribal threading appointment with this awesome woman in Turkistan. But I was still only slightly WTF until Sarah Govey who is normally unbelievably keen, cried off with a roots crisis, saying really not to worry cos Govey thinks it's too soon to describe it as toxic and Danny Fink says it will blow over in no time, but her hair was like, genuine nightmare and she'd got this precious cancellation, be mad to turn it down. And I was like, 'toxic?', 'blow over?' – and she was like OMG don't you KNOW?

And how would I because I never look at papers outside fashion week, tbh who has got the time, and

Dave always said not to bother with the News of the World because it is so desperately dry and intellectual, unless I really wanted to read page after page by Timothy Garton-Ash. So then Sarah said about Rebekah and Andy, and about everyone, even Govey, being so appallingly and shockingly misled or they would never have let me meet people like that. I mean Andy has been in our actual flat and Rebekah is still using that white Nancy tote we gave her for Christmas, Mummy says we must discontinue, asap. And apart from the sheer social death, it is such a bad look for the party and for the brand, no wonder all the envoys are hiding, total no-brainer. Mummy blames herself, since apparently everyone knows the Brookses aren't really invited anywhere in Oxfordshire, the Lord Lieutenant's wife said she would literally rather die in a ditch than eat Rebekah's nibbles. Then at last Dave came in, going I have some truly dreadful and shocking news babes – it turns out Andy was not psychic after all.

Top Gear star Jeremy Clarkson was taken for a ride by David Cameron – pretending to be the show's mystery racing driver The Stig.

The Tory leader donned the speed ace's famous white racing suit and helmet to deliver a video message to *Sun* columnist Jeremy at his fiftieth birthday bash. And Jeremy was totally taken in . . . Until Cameron whipped off the helmet to reveal the truth.

Sun, 12 April 2010

David Cameron and Rebekah Brooks are key players in what is known as the 'Chipping Norton set'. It is made up of powerful people who have become cosy neighbours in the Cotswolds, one of the most scenic parts of England. They enjoy house parties and go riding together, but their relationships run far deeper than that.

Last Christmas the Camerons, who live less than a mile away, were entertained at the home of Mrs Brooks and her second husband Charlie. Also there was James Murdoch, son of Rupert Murdoch. The meal took place just days after Mr Cameron stripped Business Secretary VincecCable of his power to decide on Mr Murdoch's BSkyB takeover.

Daily Mirror, 11 July 2011

In February 2010, the deputy editor of the *Guardian*, Ian Katz, said he telephoned Steve Hilton, Mr. Cameron's director of strategy, with some worrisome information. According to the Guardian's reporting, Mr Katz said, Mr Coulson and the *News of the World* had uncomfortably close connections to a corrupt private investigator with a criminal record named Jonathan Rees.

New York Times, 12 July 2011

David Cameron has announced that Lord Justice Leveson will lead the inquiry into phone hacking and the regulation of the media.

First Post, 13 July 2011

'Rebekah is one of my closest friends and I'm sorry but I cannot accept that she sanctioned the hacking of Milly Dowler's phone, knowing that it would cause the girl's poor parents to believe their beloved daughter was still alive ... I'd sooner believe that my mother spends her evenings working as a rent boy.'

Jeremy Clarkson, *Sun*, 16 July 2011

So it has been slightly unyay because we totally trusted
Perkins until she said she was tendering her resignation
on account of Chequers never having sunk so low, even
with the Blairs. And when Dave went calm down dear,
Harold Wilson had his moments I believe, Perkins
said that compared with Mr Coulson, Mr Kagan was a
gentleman and a scholar and she'd emigrate to Saudi
before she served that ginger hussy another Moscow
Mule, bribe or no bribe. But no hard feelings and before
she left we might want to think about that toga party,
she believed Mrs Brooks might have had her phone out,
snapping away just like she was at the Vicars 'n' Tarts,
and the Sixties Swingers, too bad nobody thought
to ask her at the time, she had seen sights in the
conservatory that would make your hair stand on end
never mind infringe your human rights, we'd be hearing
from her lawyers.

So Dave went relax babes, plenty more Perkinses in
the sea, it is at moments like this that I show my true
leadership, time for a decent party, methinks, extreme
bffs only. But our real bffs want their mobiles checked
for hackage, and all the frenemies, like the Freuds and

the Carphone-Warehouses, are bffs with Rebekah, and Andy is uber-outcast, obvs, unless he gets us the toga pictures. And Dave says Oik has got to be suspect, for planting Andy, and he's not sure about Hilto because of him being half-*Guardian*, half-Chippy, plus we're avoiding the Goveys, for now, since they are pretend or even actual bffs with Rebekah, ditto Danny the Fink who basically works for her, so sad and embarrassing.

So Dave went be cool babes, total no-brainerama, the Clarksonator will be up for it, but Clarksy went mega-gutissimo, he'd need Rebekah's permission, there was the old *Sunday Times* column to think of. Which left Helena Bonham Carter and Tim thing, since they were definitely friends at Christmas, but their number has changed and Cleggsy said he was too busy doing bathtime to go and find the new one, and Dave went no worries, Coulson would get it off Inspector Knacker, oh maybe not, how about we start a new box set? Sometimes I miss Notting Hill so much it hurts.

Knee wrinkles – or 'ninkles' as they've been christened by Vogue deputy editor Emily Sheffield – are something with which many women will be familiar: the pouchy, saggy skin and deep grooves that begin to appear on our knees from our mid-thirties.

Some of us just see it as a sign that we should sport our ninkles with pride or ditch the shorts and invest in longer skirts. But some women are so bothered by their knees that they claim they're ruining their lives.

Daily Mail, 4 July 2011

Britain's top police officer, Sir Paul Stephenson, who is under fire for hiring the former News of the World deputy editor Neil Wallis as his PR adviser, reportedly accepted 20 nights free of charge at the luxury health spa Champneys earlier this year.

Guardian, 17 July 2011

In two hours of intense questioning broken only by a bizarre incident in which Mr Murdoch was accosted with what appeared to be a foil pie plate filled with shaving cream, both he and his son James declared repeatedly that they had been shocked to discover something that has become increasingly apparent: that phone hacking and other illegal behavior were endemic at their *News of the World* tabloid, which is now defunct.

Even so, the Murdochs and Rebekah Brooks, a former editor at the paper who resigned from the News Corporation on Friday, only to be arrested on Sunday on suspicion of phone hacking and bribing the police, apologized again and again for the failures at their company.

Sarah Lyall, *New York Times*, 19 July 2011

The Chipping Norton set suddenly looks less powerful. The list of 'must attend' parties has been thrown into question. It is too early to predict how the landscape will look once all this volcanic dust has settled, but one suspects it will be permanently transformed. I have no doubt that most of Britain's PR elite will continue to flourish but, trust me, they are seriously rethinking their social calendars, alliances and strategies.

Danny Rogers, *PR Week*, 20 July 2011

So I have to write really quickly because Leveson wants the diary for his inquiry which is incredibly flattering when you think I have only been doing it for a year, as well as convenient because it is nearly full up anyway, although Anya said she would not be in any rush to buy a new one if she was me, and I was like, loving the unhesitating loyalty, girlfriend. Actually, though I will not tell Anya, I might start one of our compact mid-year 2011–2012 ones, to be on the safe side, with a matching address book because

Dave says we need to start a new one with no Chippy friends, or *Times* friends, or trusted colleagues who have let us down in a most dreadful way, he can barely look Oik in the eye. So I think we might go for something very tiny – the fuchsia panama? – which is so darling as well as completely iconic, and will not leave too much empty space. And I am sure we will soon have some new friends because the Clarksonator is going to introduce Dave to the other *Top Gear* presenters before we drop him *excited* and the Downton-Fellowes have firmly promised to have us for tea, sometime in early 2012.

But of course it has been so draining with Perkins going and fashion week looming, and everyone in Chippy going mad about house prices, when it is so unfair and not our fault if they have fallen by 30 per cent, Mummy doesn't dare set foot in Daylesford and she only met Rebekah four times. Maybe five. Plus we are still dealing with the appalling news about ninkles. Anya has the most awful case, her knees literally look like concertinas, and I may have one or two, probably from the stress. And although Dave keeps going trust your Prime Minister babes, everything will be fine, thank goodness the recess will give us some time to get help, apparently Chumpneys does this special ninkle treatment where they burn them off in an ice-chamber, and it is so brilliant because the whole Stephenson hacking thing means you can finally get an appointment. And of course the midi is back so there is, totally, hope.

Michael Ashcroft
~~The Bamfords~~ (just too uber-Chippy)
Boden
~~Rebekah and Charlie Brooks~~
Helena Bonham Carter (when I get her number)
~~Chumpneys~~
Chippy DVD
Chippy Pizza-a-go-go
~~Chippy butcher~~ – we're banned :(
~~Jeremy and Francie Clarkson~~ ???? Your call
the Cleggsies (I don't care, tbh)
~~Andy Coulson~~
~~Simon Cowell~~ – bffs with Andy
Daylesford Organic – or just too embarrassing?
~~the Dunstone Carphones~~ (unless they break with Rebekah)
Tracey Emin
~~Danny Finkelstein~~ – so loyal, I know, but the *Times*?
Julian and Emma Downton-Fellowes
~~Matthew Freud~~
Phil Green? Mummy thinks he might be toxic
~~the Govey~~
the Hagueys
~~James Harding~~

~~Steve Hilton and Rachel Whetstone~~
Anya Hindmarch
~~Hunty~~
Alex James – do we know him? Can't remember!
~~Boris Johnson~~
~~Ed Llewellyn~~
~~Will Lewis~~
Dom Loehnis – assuming Patten thing OK?
Tamara Mellon – but not if she keeps missing Farc
~~Elisabeth Murdoch~~
~~James and Kathryn Murdoch~~
~~Rupert and Wendi Murdoch~~
Ocado
Oka
~~the Oiks~~
~~Nat Rothschild~~ – or do we like him, totes forgotten!
Alice Sheffield – has not worked for you since '08
Emily Sheffield
Space NK
Isabel Spearman – it's ages since Mummy and Anya
Tommy Strathclyde – I know, but such good value
Hazey Vaizey – review after last library closes?
Whatever – you <u>must</u> tell me his real name!

Acknowledgements

would like to thank the *Guardian*'s Emily Wilson and Clare
Margetson for commissioning 'Mrs Cameron's Diaries', and
e excellent *G2* editorial team for looking after them each
k. Thank you also to Ursula Doyle of Virago for thinking
the book and to her colleague, Victoria Pepe for editing
My friend Jill Hollis generously found time to subject
various entries to a North of the Border comprehensibility
test, and my daughter Frances Bennett kindly policed the
slang.

Catherine Bennett is a British journalist, working for the *Observer* as a columnist, and also contributing to the *Guardian*, in which 'Mrs Cameron's Diary' appears. She grew up in Leeds, read English at Oxford, then worked in London for publications including the *Sunday Telegraph*, the *Mail on Sunday*, *Vogue*, *Elle*, the *Sunday Times*, the *Times* and the short-lived *Sunday Correspondent*. She has written and presented documentaries for BBC 4. She joined the *Guardian* in 1990 and moved to its sister paper, the *Observer*, in 2008. She has also written as Norman Johnson, Will Duguid and former Labour MP, Ron Scuttle. Catherine Bennett lives in North London.